The Little TMMi

Objective-Driven Test Process Improvement

The Little TMMi

Objective-Driven

Test Process Improvement

Erik van Veenendaal

Jan Jaap Cannegieter

UTN Publishers   's-Hertogenbosch 2011

Trademarks

The following registered trademarks and service marks are used in this book: CMM®, CMMI®, IDEAL℠, ISTQB®, PRISMA®, TMap®, TMap NEXT®, TPI®, TPI-NEXT®, TMM℠ and TMMi®.

CMM and CMMI are registered in the U.S. Patent and Trademark Office by Carnegie Mellon University, USA.

IDEAL are service marks of Carnegie Mellon University, USA.

ISTQB is a registered trademark of the International Software Testing Qualification Board, Belgium.

PRISMA is a registered trademark of Improve Quality Services, The Netherlands.

TMap, TMap NEXT, TPI and TPI-NEXT are registered trademarks of Sogeti, The Netherlands.

TMM is a registered service mark of Illinois Institute of Technology, USA.

TMMi is a registered trademark of TMMi Foundation, Ireland.

UTN Publishers
Willem van Oranjelaan 5
5211 CN 's-Hertogenbosch
The Netherlands
www.utn.nl

ISBN 9789490986032

Contents

Foreword

I have been very lucky to have been involved in TMMi since it was initiated. When we started out on the journey of developing a standard reference model for test and quality we had no idea how popular this would be. We were just a few consultants concerned that there was no standard approach to test assessment and, therefore, clients were simply at the mercy of the quality and experience of the consultant they employed when they wanted to understand how good their process was. It was also the case that the reviews undertaken where not repeatable stopping any ongoing measurement of improvements. TMMi, owned and managed by the TMMi Foundation, now provides the first non-commercial assessment model. The foundation provides a common test model and TAMAR (TMMi Assessment Method Accreditation Requirements) to ensure consistent implementation and results from a test process assessment.

It is very fitting, therefore, that although the initial concept of a maturity model for testing was developed in the US, the first book based upon the new TMMi model should have been initially published in The Netherlands, where most often in recent years step changes in software testing have originated. Now with its growing popularity it is pleasing to see it translated into English opening the contents to a far wider audience.

The content is clear and easy to read and understand. I know this book will be successful in helping many test engineers and test managers to understand the TMMi model and how they can change the testing process in a controlled and successful way.

Improving software testing and quality is the way forward for all of us if we hope to stop all of those high profile software disasters that regularly appear on the news. Unless we approach things differently, nothing will change; this book will be an invaluable companion on that journey.

After reading this book I hope you too will see the benefits of using TMMi.

Geoff Thompson
Chair – TMMi Management Executive

Preface

Welcome to *The Little TMMi – Objective-Driven Test Process Improvement*. TMMi is a non-commercial, organization-independent test maturity model. With TMMi, organizations can have their test processes objectively evaluated by certified assessors, improve their test processes and even have their test process and test organization formally accredited if it complies with the requirements. The main advantages of TMMi over other test improvement models are independence, the alignment with international standards, the business-orientation (objective-driven) and the perfect match with the CMMI-framework.

TMMi Foundation
TMMi has been developed by the TMMi Foundation, a non-profit organization based in Dublin (Ireland) that has as main objectives to develop and maintain the TMMi model, create a benchmark database and facilitate formal assessment by accredited lead assessors. Testers can (free of charge) become a member of the TMMi Foundation, and from that membership a board is being elected. Many international test experts have contributed to the current version of TMMi. It has already proven to be highly useful in practice. Many organizations world-wide are already using TMMi for their internal test improvement process. Other organizations already have formally achieved TMMi level 2 and even TMMi level 3.

Advantages of TMMi
TMMi is aligned with international testing standards such as IEEE and the syllabi and terminology of the International Software Testing Qualifications Board (ISTQB). The TMMi Foundation has consciously not introduced new or their own terminology, but re-uses the ISTQB terminology. This is an advantage for all those test professionals who are ISTQB certified (approximately 170.000 world-wide at the time of this publishing). TMMi also differs from other test improvement models by being business-driven.

Testing is never an activity on its own. By introducing the process area Test Policy and Goals already at TMMi level 2, testing becomes aligned with organizational and quality objectives early in the improvement model. It should be clear to all stakeholders why there is a need to improve as well as an understanding of the business case. A final difference between TMMi and other test improvement models is the conformity of TMMi to the CMMI framework. The structure and the generic components of CMMI have been re-used within TMMi. This has two main advantages: first, the structure already has been shown in practice to be successful and, second, organizations that use CMMI are already familiar with the structure and terminology which makes it easier to accept TMMi and simplifies the application of TMMi in these organizations.

Target Audience
The Little TMMi has been written to address a large target audience. Testers and test managers can use it to evaluate and improve their processes. Test consultants can use it during assessments of test improvement projects. Other stakeholders can use it to acquire testing knowledge in general and TMMi knowledge in particular. CMMI consultants and QA employees can, by means of this compact publication, relatively easily become familiar with a test improvement model that is compliant with CMMI.

Content
The book does not contain a full and detailed description of TMMi. The model is described at a higher level as are the goals and practices per process area, including a specific list of supporting literature to be used when one wants to improve a certain test process. The way assessments are performed and the implementation of TMMi are also discussed. The book also contains a number of appendices, including a table explaining the relationship with CMMI, a glossary and an index list.

The full TMMi model can be found at the web site of the TMMi Foundation: www.TMMifoundation.org. In this first edition of *The Little TMMi*, the TMMi framework version 3.1 is used. This implies that the TMMi model and levels 2 to 5 are described. However, for TMMi level 5 only the goals are described. The full description, including practices is expected to be published in mid 2011. The authors have decided to publish *The Little TMMi* now, since it allows organizations to start using TMMi level 2, 3 and 4. In a future edition the practices of TMMi level 5 will be described.

Acknowledgments
Many people reviewed the draft versions of this book, and also the earlier published Dutch version [Van Veenendaal/Cannegieter]. We would like to thank explicitly the following people (in alphabetical order): Frans van Asten, Bryan Bakker, Bart Bouwers, Bart Fessl, Pascal Maus, Judy McKay, Fran O'Hara, Manfred van Roekel, Geoff Thompson, Brian Wells and Johan Zandhuis.

Our objective is to support (test) organizations in improving their test process, to expand the adoption of TMMi and to enhance the growth of the testing profession. We wish you lots of success.

Erik van Veenendaal
Jan Jaap Cannegieter

1 Introduction

1.1 Background

For the past decade, the software industry has invested substantial effort to improve the quality of its products. This has been a difficult job, since the size and complexity of software increases rapidly while customers and users are becoming more and more demanding. Despite encouraging results with various quality improvement approaches, the software industry is still far from zero defects. To improve product quality, the software industry has often focused on improving its development processes.

A guideline that has been widely used to improve the development processes is the Capability Maturity Model [Paulk]. The Capability Maturity Model (CMM) and its successor, the Capability Maturity Model Integration (CMMI), are often regarded as the industry standard for software process improvement. The CMM provided process improvement projects with the necessary structure and direction. CMM became a model to determine how mature the organization is, or as Watts Humphrey likes to state: "If you don't know where you are, a map won't help." However, for the testing community, CMM was insufficient. Despite the fact that testing often accounts for at least 30-40% of the total project costs, only limited attention is given to testing in the CMM. At maturity level 3 of the CMM there are some requirements for the testing process, but these are of such a high level of abstraction that they are hardly usable in practice.

The successor of the CMM, the Capability Maturity Model Integration for Development (CMMI) [CMMI DEV] has two dedicated process areas (verification and validation) that provide more focus on testing. Still CMMI has too few practical tools to support a step by step improvement of the testing process. The emphasis of CMMI is on organizational, and software and system engineering processes and not so much on the characteristics of a mature testing process. As an answer, the TMMi Foundation has created its own improvement model: the Test Maturity Model integration (TMMi). TMMi is a detailed model for test process improvement and is positioned as being complementary to CMMI.

1.2 The Test Maturity Model integration

Origin and Structure
The TMMi framework has been developed by the TMMi Foundation as a guideline and reference framework for test process improvement and is

positioned as a complementary model to CMMI Version 1.2 [CMMI DEV], addressing those issues important to test managers, test engineers and software quality professionals. Testing as defined in the TMMi is applied in its broadest sense to encompass all software product quality-related activities.

> **Testing:** *The process consisting of all lifecycle activities, both static and dynamic, concerned with planning, preparation and evaluation of software products and related work products to determine that they satisfy specified requirements, to demonstrate that they are fit for purpose and to detect defects. [ISTQB Glossary]*

Just like the CMMI staged representation, TMMi also uses the concept of maturity levels for process evaluation and improvement. Furthermore process areas, goals and practices are identified. Applying the TMMi maturity criteria will improve the test process and have a positive impact on product quality, test engineering productivity, and cycle-time effort. TMMi has been developed to support organizations with evaluating and improving their test process.

Practical experiences are positive and show that TMMi supports the process of establishing a more effective and efficient test process. By following the TMMi guidelines, testing becomes a profession and a fully integrated part of the development process. As stated, the focus of testing changes from defect detection to defect prevention.

Advantages

The application of TMMi will lead to a structured and controlled test process, a higher level of product quality, improved productivity of the test organization and, frequently, a shorter lead time. This will be discussed in more detail in Section 1.4. TMMi has been developed to support organizations to evaluate and improve their test processes. Within TMMi testing moves from a chaotic, unstructured process with a shortage of skilled testers and tools, to a mature and controlled process that has defect prevention as its main objective.

Scope

TMMi is intended to support testing activities and test process improvement in both the systems engineering and software engineering disciplines. Systems engineering covers the development of total systems, which may or may not include software. Software engineering covers the development of software systems.

Whereas some models for test process improvement focus mainly on high-level testing, e.g., Test Process Improvement (TPI) [Koomen/Pol] and its successor TPI-NEXT [Sogeti], or address only one aspect of structured testing e.g., the test organization, TMMi addresses all test levels (including static testing) and aspects of structured testing. With respect to dynamic testing, both lower test levels (e.g., component test, integration test) and higher test levels (e.g., system test, acceptance test) are within the scope of TMMi. Studying the model more in detail one will learn that the model addresses all four cornerstones for structured testing (lifecycle, techniques, infrastructure and organization) [TMap].

1.3 Sources

Capability Maturity Model Integration (CMMI)
The development of TMMi has used the TMM framework as developed by the Illinois Institute of Technology as one of its major sources [Burnstein]. In addition to the TMM, it was largely guided by the work done on the Capability Maturity Model Integration (CMMI), a process improvement model that has widespread support in the IT industry. CMMI has both a staged and continuous representation. Within the staged representation the CMMI architecture prescribes the stages that an organization must proceed through in an orderly fashion to improve its development process. Within the continuous representation there is no fixed set of levels or stages to proceed through. An organization applying the continuous representation can select areas for improvement from many different categories.

TMMi has been developed as a staged model. The staged model uses predefined sets of process areas to define an improvement path for an organization. This improvement path is described by a model component called a maturity level. A maturity level is a well-defined evolutionary plateau towards achieving improved organizational processes. Within TMMi each maturity level has a structure in which process areas, goals and practices are defined.

CMMI was considered during the naming and definition of the components of the TMMi framework and during the elaboration of some process areas. Both TMMi and CMMI make use the inheritance principle: all requirements of the underlying level(s) need to be complied with, to be able to start with the next level. TMMi is comparable to CMMI in terms of its framework structure and is complementary to CMMI in its focus on the testing process. The TMMi Foundation has stated that at a later stage a continuous version may also be developed. It is expected that this will most likely not change the (testing) content of the model but will influence the framework structure and representation.

The TMMi Foundation has positioned TMMi as a complementary model to CMMI. In many cases a TMMi level that one aims to achieve needs specific support from CMMI process areas at a similar or lower level. In some cases support is needed from a process area at a higher CMMI level (see appendix A). Process areas and activities that are described in detail in CMMI are generally not again described in TMMi but are just referenced. An example is the CMMI process area Configuration Management. Of course configuration management is also applicable on test deliverables (testware); however, this topic is not elaborated upon in detail in TMMi. Instead, the configuration management practices from CMMI are referenced and implicitly re-used. An exception to this rule is made for peer reviews. Peer reviews are present both in CMMI (as part of the Verification process area) and TMMi (as a dedicated process area) as one also needs to able to use TMMi as an independent test improvement model. Other sources to TMMi development include Gelperin and Hetzel's evolutionary testing model [Gelperin and Hetzel], which describes the evolution of the testing process over a 40-year period, Beizer's testing model, which describes the evolution of the individual tester's thinking [Beizer], research on the TMM carried out in the EU-funded MB-TMM project, and international testing standards, e.g., IEEE 829 Standard for Software Test Documentation [IEEE 829]. The testing terminology used in TMMi is derived from the ISTQB Standard Glossary of Terms Used in Software Testing [ISTQB Glossary].

Evolutionary Testing Model

The first phase in Gelperin and Hetzel's evolutionary testing model is identified as "debugging-oriented". During this phase, which can be compared to TMMi level 1, the software organization does not distinguish between testing and debugging. Testing is perceived as a debugging activity. The objective of testing is to ensure that the software runs without major failures.

In the subsequent "demonstration-oriented" phase, testing is separated from debugging. Both activities have their own objectives: debugging needs to ensure that the software runs whereas testing needs to ensure the software complies with its requirements specification. During the "demonstration-oriented" phase test planning and test design techniques are introduced in the organization. However, testing becomes involved and starts relatively late in a project. This phase and the subsequent "destruction-oriented" phase have a strong correlation to TMMi level 2. In the "destruction-oriented" phase, testing is perceived as an activity to find defects. The statements "there are always defects" and "defect-free software does not exist" are used to set the mind. The objective "ensure that the software complies to the requirements specification", is emphatically enhanced with so-called negative testing. Negative testing is defined as "Tests aimed at showing that a component or system does not work"

[ISTQB Glossary]. Negative testing is related to the tester's attitude rather than a specific test approach or test design technique, e.g., testing with invalid input values or exceptions.

During the "evaluation-oriented" phase, testing is fully integrated in the software development lifecycle. Testing is now a process that starts early in a project. The scope of testing is enhanced to include finding defects in documentation (e.g., requirements specifications) by defining reviews to be part of testing. All activities that are concerned with finding defects are perceived to be part of the test process. The objective of testing is providing (quantitative) visibility into the quality of the product. The "evaluation-oriented" phase can be linked to elements from TMMi level 3 and partly to TMMi level 4. The evolutionary testing model is completed by means of the "prevention-oriented" phase, comparable to TMMi level 5. During this phase, testing is a completely defined and controlled process. The focus of testing is no longer on finding defects, but rather on the prevention of defects, in both the product and in the process. Testing activities such as reviews, test planning and test design are focused around this advanced objective. New testing practices such as causal analysis are introduced into the organization at this phase.

The correlation between the evolutionary testing model and the TMMi levels is shown in Table 1.1.

Table 1.1 Relationship between evolutionary testing model and TMMi	
Evolutionary testing model	**TMMi**
Prevention-oriented phase	level 5 Optimization
Evaluation-oriented phase	level 4 Measured level 3 Defined
Destruction-oriented phase Demonstration-oriented phase	level 2 Managed
Debugging-oriented phase	level 1 Initial

1.4 The Costs and Benefits of TMMi

Executing an improvement program using TMMi demands an investment. When speaking about costs and benefits of TMMi usually a distinction is made between direct and indirect costs and benefits. Direct costs and benefits can directly be allocated to the improvement program and can be expressed in terms of money. Examples of direct costs are effort (work hours), training and education and external consultancy. Examples of direct benefits are a rise in productivity, less interruptions during production and less damage repair because defects were found at earlier stages in the process. Indirect costs and benefits cannot directly be allocated to the improvement program or are more difficult to express in terms of money. Examples of indirect costs are the time spent in training, the learning curve caused by job rotations and productivity loss because of opposition to the process changes. Examples of indirect benefits are the improvement in staff motivation, increased loyalty from customers, higher interchangeability of employees and an improvement in the working environment.

In practice often only the direct costs and benefits are taken into account in a Return on Investment (ROI) calculation. On the one hand this is understandable because these metrics are easier to determine than the indirect costs and benefits. On the other hand the indirect benefits are sometimes larger or even more important than the direct ones. Therefore, it is better to try to take into account indirect benefits when the added value of a TMMi improvement program is being determined. Because investments in process improvement need long term management support, it is crucial to measure the return of an improvement program accurately and consistently.

As TMMi is a relatively recent model, the number of publications about costs and benefits in practice is limited. However, to give a certain insight into the costs and benefits, an overview of proven figures for improvement programs is shown in Table 1.2. Keep in mind that these are mainly numbers of CMM(I) improvement programs. The table has been included under the assumption that TMMi improvement programs take place under relatively the same conditions and are expected to yield similar results.

Table 1.2 Metrics of improvement programs [Van Solingen]			
SPI-metrics	**Real minimum value**	**Real maximum value**	**Average value**
Costs			
Financial expenditure per employee	€ 1.000	€ 5.000	€ 2.500
Time spent per employee	1%	5%	3%
Returns			
Financial rating per employee	€ 5.000	€ 55.000	€ 20.000
Return On Investment	4	10	7

It is often said that the profits of process improvement are difficult to measure. Most organizations find it relatively simple to measure the costs, but more difficult to measure the profits. The direct profits of TMMi are often measured by comparing the old situation, the one before the implementation of TMMi, to the new situation. Indirect profits, such as "increase in customer satisfaction" or "increase in personnel motivation", can be measured by conducting interviews or using questionnaires.

As said before, explicitly measuring costs and benefits of a TMMi investment is important. This guarantees the continuity of the improvement program and also stimulates the commitment of both management and employees. To illustrate the possible outcomes (returns), some results of organizations that conducted a TMMi improvement program in which one of the authors was involved are shown below. An IT organization that ultimately reached TMMi level 3, as one of the first testing organizations worldwide, reported results in shortening the completion time of the test execution phase (Graph 1.1) and a higher Defect Detection Percentage (DDP) during the system test (Graph 1.2). Here Defect Detection Percentage has been defined as "the number of defects found by a test phase, divided by the number found by that test phase and any other means afterwards" [ISTQB Glossary of Terms].

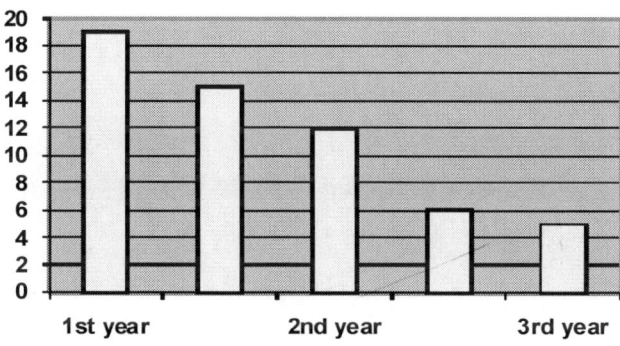

Graph 1.1: System test execution time in weeks

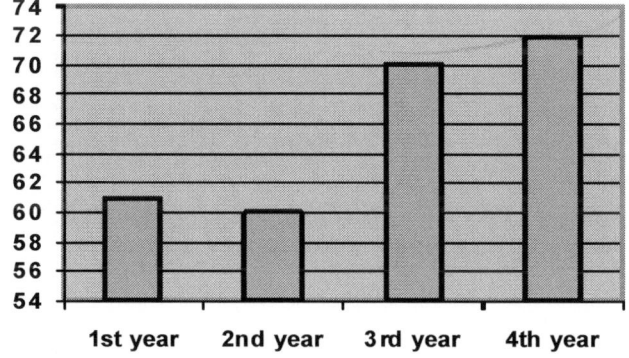

Graph 1.2: Defect Detection Percentage

After a certain amount of time almost every organization reports better predictability of the testing process. An example of this can be seen in Graph 1.3, also from a report of an IT organization at TMMi level 2. Initially around 100% deviation (and more), but after spending on test process improvement deviation was more under control and within 20%. Lastly, Graph 1.4 was taken from a report of a financial organization on its way toward TMMi level 2. It clearly shows the improvement of the Defect Detection Percentage during the system test.

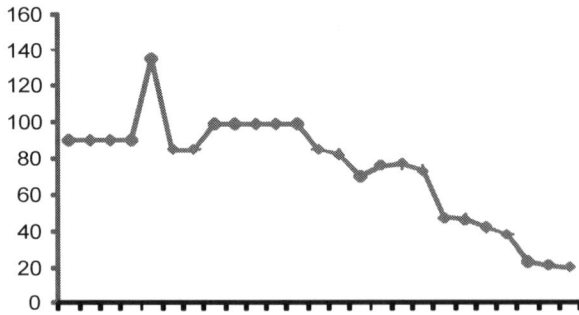

Graph 1.3: Deviation of test time spent versus estimated test time (percentage)

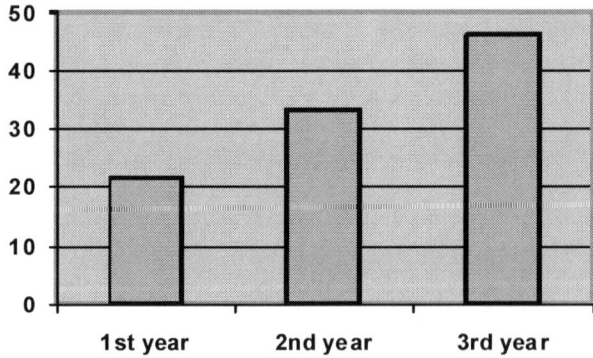

Graph 1.4: Defect Detection Percentage of the system test

2 TMMi: The Model

2.1 Overview

TMMi has a staged architecture for process improvement. It contains stages or levels through which an organization passes as its testing process evolves from one that is ad hoc and unmanaged to one that is managed, defined, measured, and optimized. Achieving each stage ensures that all goals of that stage have been achieved and the improvements form the foundation for the next stage.

The internal structure of TMMi is rich in testing practices that can be learned and applied in a systematic way to support a quality testing process that improves in incremental steps. There are five levels in TMMi that prescribe the maturity hierarchy and the evolutionary path to test process improvement. Each level has a set of process areas that an organization must implement to achieve maturity at that level.

Experience has shown that organizations do their best when they focus their test process improvement efforts on a manageable number of process areas at a time, and that those areas require increasing sophistication as the organization improves. Because each maturity level forms a necessary foundation for the next level, trying to skip a maturity level or a process area is usually counterproductive. At the same time, it is important to recognize that test process improvement efforts should focus on the needs of the organization in the context of its business environment and the process areas at higher maturity levels may address the current needs of an organization or project. For example, organizations seeking to move from maturity level 1 to maturity level 2 are frequent encouraged to establish a test group, which is addressed by the Test Organization process area that resides at maturity level 3. Although the test group is not a necessary characteristic of a TMMi level 2 organization, it can be a useful part of the organization's approach to achieve TMMi maturity level 2.

The process areas for each maturity level of TMMi are shown in Figure 2.1. They are fully described later in other chapters and are also listed below along with a brief description of the characteristics of an organization at each TMMi level. The description introduces the reader to the evolutionary path prescribed in TMMi for test process improvement.

Note that TMMi does not have a specific process area dedicated to test tools and/or test automation. Within TMMi test tools are treated as a supporting resource (practice) and are therefore part of the process area

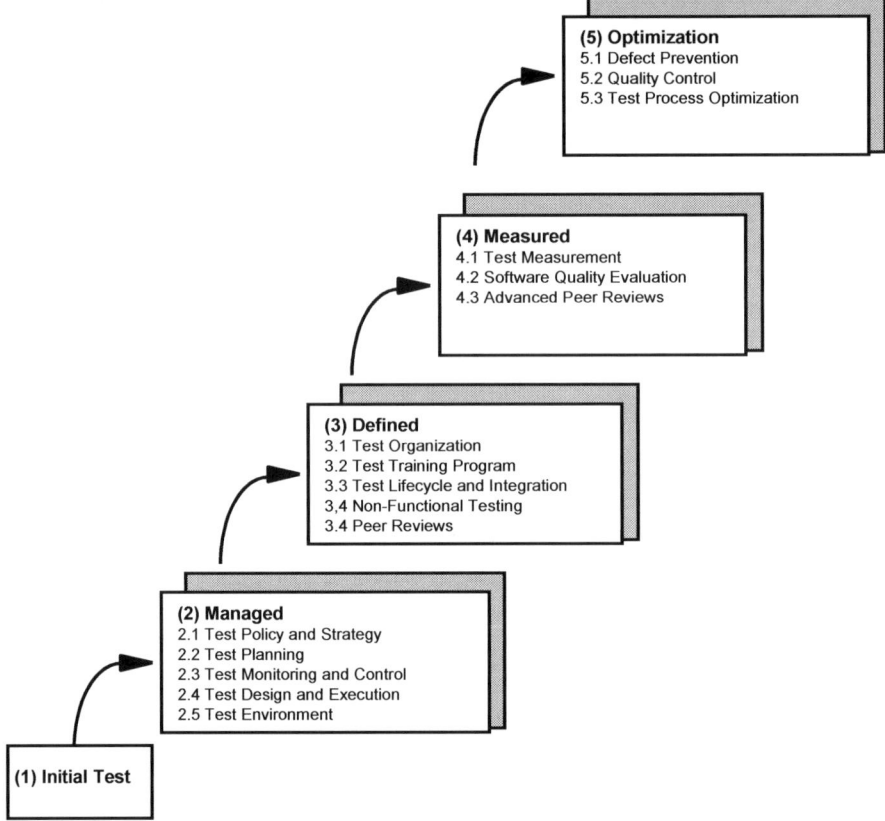

Figure 2.1: TMMi maturity levels and process areas

where they provide support, e.g., applying a test design tool is a supporting test practice within the process area Test Design and Execution at TMMi level 2 and applying a performance testing tool is a supporting test practice within the process area Non-Functional Testing at TMMi level 3.

2.2 The TMMi Maturity Levels

2.2.1 Level 1 - Initial

At TMMi level 1, testing is a chaotic, undefined process and is often considered a part of debugging. The organization usually does not provide a stable environment to support the testing. Success in these organizations depends on the competence and heroics of the people in the organization and not the use of proven processes. Tests are developed in an ad hoc way after coding is completed. Testing and debugging are interleaved to get the bugs out of the system. The objective of testing at this level is to show that the software runs without major failures. Products are released without adequate visibility regarding quality and risks. In the field, the product often does not fulfill its needs, is not stable, and/or is too slow. Within testing there is a lack of resources, tools and well-educated staff. At TMMi level 1 there are no defined process areas. Maturity level 1 organizations are characterized by a tendency to over commit, abandonment of processes in a time of crises, and an inability to repeat their successes. In addition products tend not to be released on time, budgets are overrun and delivered quality is not according to expectations.

2.2.2 Level 2 - Managed

At TMMi level 2, testing becomes a managed process and is clearly separated from debugging. The process discipline reflected by maturity level 2 helps to ensure that existing practices are retained during times of stress. However, testing is still perceived by many stakeholders as being a project phase that follows coding.

In the context of improving the test process, a company-wide or program-wide test strategy is established. Test plans are also developed. Within the test plan a test approach is defined that is based on the result of a product risk assessment. Risk management techniques are used to identify the product risks based on documented requirements. The test plan defines what testing is required, when, how and by whom. Commitments are established with stakeholders and revised as needed. Testing is monitored and controlled to ensure it is proceeding according to plan and actions can be taken when deviations occur. The status of the work products and the delivery of testing services are visible to management. Test design techniques are applied for deriving and selecting test cases from specifications. However, testing may still start relatively late in the development lifecycle, e.g., during the design or even during the coding phase.

In TMMI level 2 testing is multi-leveled: there are component, integration, system and acceptance test levels. For each identified test level there are specific testing objectives defined in the organization-wide or program-wide test strategy.

The main objective of testing in a TMMi level 2 organization is to verify that the product satisfies the specified requirements. Many quality problems at this TMMi level occur because testing occurs late in the development lifecycle. Defects are propagated from the requirements and design into the code. There are no formal review programs at this level to address this important issue. Post code, execution-based testing is still considered by many stakeholders the primary testing activity.

The process areas at TMMi level 2 are:
　2.1 Test Policy and Strategy
　2.2 Test Planning
　2.3 Test Monitoring and Control
　2.4 Test Design and Execution
　2.5 Test Environment

2.2.3　Level 3 - Defined

At TMMi level 3, testing is no longer confined to a phase that follows coding. It is fully integrated into the development lifecycle and the associated milestones. Test planning is done at an early project stage, e.g., during the requirements phase, and is documented in a master test plan. The development of a master test plan builds on the test planning skills and commitments acquired at TMMi level 2. The organization's set of standard test processes, which is the basis for maturity level 3, is established and improved over time. A test organization and a specific test training program exist, and testing is perceived as being a profession. Test process improvement is fully institutionalized as part of the test organization's accepted practices.

Organizations at level 3 understand the importance of reviews in building a quality product; a formal review program is implemented but is not fully linked to the dynamic testing process at this level. Reviews take place throughout the lifecycle. Test professionals are involved in reviews of the requirements specifications. Whereby the test designs at TMMi level 2 focus mainly on functional testing, test designs and test techniques are expanded at level 3 to include non-functional testing, e.g., usability and/or reliability, depending on the business objectives.

A critical distinction between TMMi maturity level 2 and 3 is the scope of the standards, process descriptions, and procedures. At maturity level 2 these may be quite different in each specific instance, e.g., on a particular project or for a particular team. At maturity level 3 these are tailored from the organization's set of standard processes to suit a particular project or organizational unit and, therefore, are more consistent except for the differences allowed by the tailoring guidelines. Another critical distinction is that at maturity level 3, processes are typically described more rigorously than at maturity level 2. As a consequence, at maturity level 3 the organization must revisit the maturity level 2 process areas and may need to refine the defined processes.

The process areas at TMMi level 3 are:
  3.1 Test Organization
  3.2 Test Training Program
  3.3 Test Lifecycle and Integration
  3.4 Non-Functional Testing
  3.5 Peer Reviews

2.2.4   Level 4 - Measured

Achieving the goals of TMMi level 2 and 3 has the benefits of putting into place a technical, managerial, and staffing infrastructure capable of thorough testing and providing support for test process improvement. With this infrastructure established, testing can become a measured process to encourage further growth and accomplishment. In TMMi level 4 organizations, testing is a thoroughly defined, well-founded and measurable process. Testing is perceived as evaluation; it consists of all lifecycle activities concerned with checking products and related work products.

At this level, an organization-wide test measurement program is put into place that is used to evaluate the quality of the testing process, to assess productivity, and to monitor improvements. Measures are incorporated into the organization's measurement repository to support fact-based decision making. The test measurement program also supports evaluation of test work products and predictions relating to test performance and cost.

With respect to product quality, the presence of a measurement program allows an organization to implement a product quality evaluation process by defining quality needs, quality attributes and quality metrics. Products are evaluated using quantitative criteria for quality attributes such as reliability, usability and maintainability. Product quality is understood in quantitative terms and is managed to the defined objectives throughout the lifecycle.

Reviews and inspections are considered to be part of testing and are used to measure product quality early in the lifecycle and to formally control quality gates. Peer review as a defect detection technique transforms into a product quality measurement technique in line with the process area Product Quality Evaluation.

TMMi level 4 also covers establishing a coordinated test approach between peer reviews (static testing) and dynamic testing and using peer review results and data to optimize the test approach, both with the goal of making testing more effective and more efficient. Peer reviews are now fully integrated with the dynamic testing process, e.g., part of the test strategy, test plan and test approach.

The process areas at TMMi level 4 are:
4.1 Test Measurement
4.2 Product Quality Evaluation
4.3 Advanced Peer Reviews

2.2.5 Level 5 - Optimization

The achievement of all previous test improvement goals at levels 1 through 4 of TMMi has created an organizational infrastructure for testing that supports a completely defined and measured process. At TMMi maturity level 5, an organization is capable of continually improving its processes based on a quantitative understanding of statistically controlled processes. Improving test process performance is carried out through incremental and innovative process and technological improvements. The testing methods and techniques are optimized and there is a continuous focus on fine-tuning and process improvement. An optimized test process, as defined by the TMMi is one that is:

- Managed, defined, measured, efficient and effective
- Statistically controlled and predictable
- Focused on defect prevention
- Supported by automation as much as is deemed an effective use of resources
- Able to support technology transfer from the industry to the organization
- Able to support re-use of test assets
- Focused on process change to achieve continuous improvement.

To support the continuous improvement of the test process infrastructure, and to identify, plan and implement test improvements, a permanent test process improvement group is formally established and is staffed by members who have received specialized training to increase the level of their skills and knowledge required for the success of the group. In many organizations this group is called a Test Process Group (TPG). Support for a TPG formally begins at TMMi level 3 when the test organization is introduced. At TMMi level 4 and 5, the responsibilities grow as more high level practices are introduced, e.g., identifying reusable test (process) assets and developing and maintaining the test (process) asset library.

The Defect Prevention process area is established to identify and analyze common causes of defects across the development lifecycle and define actions to prevent similar defects from occurring in the future. Outliers to test process performance, as identified as part of process quality control, are analyzed to address their causes as part of Defect Prevention.

The test process is now statistically managed by means of the Quality Control process area. Statistical sampling, measurements of confidence levels, trustworthiness, and reliability drive the test process. The test process is characterized by sampling-based quality measurements.

At TMMi level 5, the Test Process Optimization process area introduces mechanisms to fine-tune and continuously improve testing. There is an established procedure to identify process enhancements as well as to select and evaluate new testing technologies. Tools support the test process as much as is effective during test design, test execution, regression testing, test case management, defect collection and analysis, etc. Process and test-ware re-use across the organization is also common practice and is supported by a test (process) asset library.

The three TMMi level 5 process areas, Defect Prevention, Quality Control and Test Process Optimization all provide support for continuous process improvement. In fact, the three process areas are highly interrelated. For example, Defect Prevention supports Quality Control, e.g., by analyzing outliers to process performance and by implementing practices for defect causal analysis and prevention of defect re-occurrence. Quality Control contributes to Test Process Optimization, and Test Process Optimization supports both Defect Prevention and Quality Control, for example by implementing the test improvement proposals. All of these process areas are, in turn, supported by the practices that were acquired when the lower-level process areas were implemented. At TMMi level 5, testing is a process with the objective of preventing defects.

Process areas at TMMi level 5 are:
    5.1 Defect Prevention
    5.2 Test Process Optimization
    5.3 Quality Control.

2.3 The Structure of a Process Area

The generic structure of a TMMi process area is shown in Figure 2.2.

Informative Components
Every process area has a number of informative components (purpose, introduction, scope). Informative components provide details that help organizations get started in thinking about how to approach the required and expected components. Other examples of information model compo-

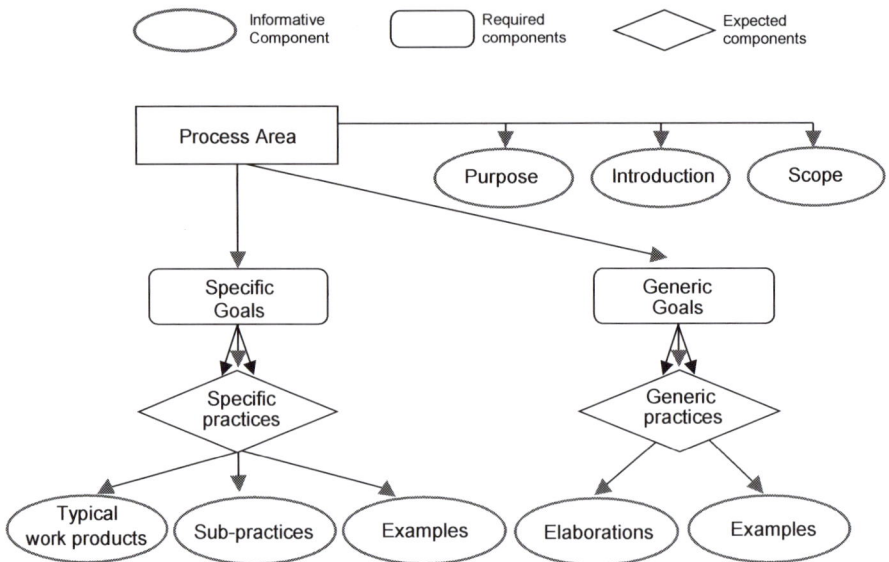

Figure 2.2: Structure of a TMMi process area

nents are sub-practices and typical work products. The purposes of the process areas are described in Chapter 3. The introduction and scope components for each process area are not provided in this book. These can be found in the full TMMi document (www.TMMifoundation.org).

Goals

Each process area has two types of goals: generic goals and specific goals. The generic goals are the same for each process area. A generic goal describes the characteristics that must be present to institutionalize the processes that implement a process area. When a process is fully institutionalized the process is perceived as being followed naturally by the organization and its employees even when under time-pressure. In addition to generic goals, every process area also has a number of specific goals that are specific to the process area. A specific goal describes a unique characteristic that must be present to satisfy the process area. For example, Perform a Product Risk Assessment is a specific goal of the Test Planning process area and Establish Test Functions for Test Specialists is a specific goal of the Test Organization process area.

Practices

Practices are recommendations for how a goal can be achieved. The specific goals are elaborated by means of specific practices and the generic goals are elaborated by means of generic practices. Examples of specific practices related to the specific goal Perform a Product Risk Assessment are

Define product risk categories and parameters and Identify product risks. Examples of generic practices related to the generic goal Institutionalize a Managed Process are Plan the process and Assign responsibilities. The specific goals, specific practices, generic goals and generic practices are described in Chapter 3.

Sub-practices, Typical Work Products

The generic and specific practices are supported by informative components such as sub-practices, typical work products and examples. These informative components support the understanding of the practice and make it concrete. The informative components of TMMi are not provided in this book. These can be found in the full TMMi document (www.TMMifoundation.org).

Required, Expected and Informative Components

The various components of a process area have different meanings. The specific and generic goals are required components. Required components describe what an organization must achieve to satisfy a process area. This achievement must be visibly and consistently implemented in an organization's processes.

The practices are expected components. Expected components describe what an organization will typically implement to achieve a required component. Either the practices as described or acceptable alternatives to the practices must be present in the planned and implemented processes of the organization, before goals can be considered satisfied.

The only formal requirements are the goals; these must be satisfied. The practices are a recommended way to achieve the goals. The informative components are for information only and formally do not have the status of a required or expected component. Informative components provide details that help organizations get started in thinking about how to approach the required and expected components.

2.4 Generic Components and Their Correlation with Specific Components

As explained in Section 2.3, generic goals and generic practices are applicable to all process areas. The generic goals comprise the characteristics that must be present to institutionalize the processes that implement a process area. An institutionalized process is an ingrained way of doing business that an organization follows routinely as part of its corporate culture. With an institutionalized process, the employees who execute the process perceive it as the standard way of working, there is commitment from management to this way of working and the process is executed consistently. The process is also followed in times of stress (e.g. time-pressure).

TMMi recognizes two levels of institutionalization described in two generic goals: generic goal 2 and generic goal 3. Note that generic goal 1 of CMMI, Achieve Specific Goals, not taken into account since this only relates to the continuous representation of CMMI and therefore has no relevance to the staged representation of TMMi. The same reasoning applies to the CMMI generic goals 4 and 5; these generic goals also only related to a continuous representation and therefore not relevant to the staged representation of the TMMi. As with the specific goals, the generic goals are elaborated upon by means of generic practices.

Generic goal 2 ensures the institutionalization of a managed process. A managed process is a process that accomplishes the work necessary to produce work products. It is planned and executed in accordance with policy, employs skilled people and has adequate resources to produce controlled outputs. A managed process involves relevant stakeholders, is monitored and controlled, is subjected to reviews and is evaluated for adherence to its process descriptions. The process may be instantiated by a project, group, or organizational unit. The implementation of the processes in line with generic goal 2 can differ per project. Institutionalization of the processes occurs at the project level.

Generic goal 2 also ensures the institutionalization of a defined process. A defined process has maintained process descriptions and contributes work products, measures, and other process improvement information to the organizational process assets. A critical distinction between a managed process and a defined process is the scope of application of the process descriptions, standards, and procedures. For a managed process, descriptions, standards, and procedures are applicable to a particular project, group, or organizational function. As a result, the managed processes of two projects in one organization may be different. A defined process is standardized as much as possible across the organization and adapted only when required for a specific project or organizational function based on the tailoring guidelines. Both generic goal 2 and generic goal 3 are elaborated upon in Chapter 3.

The capability level being targeted will determine which generic goals and practices are applicable. When trying to reach maturity level 2 the process areas at maturity level 2 as well as generic goal 2 and the accompanying generic practices are applicable. As stated, the implementation at TMMi level 2 can differ per project. Generic goal 3 is only applicable when trying to reach maturity level 3 or higher. This means that after achieving a maturity level 2 rating, to achieve a maturity level 3 rating the organization must revisit the maturity level 2 process areas and apply generic goal 3 and the accompanying practices to each of those process areas. In practice this means that all TMMi level 2 process areas must be re-defined to define an organization-wide approach and implement it. This is summarized and presented in Table 2.1.

Table 2.1 Process areas, specific goals and generic goals				
Process area	Maturity level	Specific Goals	Generic Goal GG2	Generic Goal GG3
Test Policy and Test Strategy	2	Objective maturity level 2		
Test Planning	2			
Test Monitoring and Control	2			
Test Design and Execution	2			
Test Environment	2			
Test Organization	3	Objective maturity level 3		
Test Training Program	3			
Test Lifecycle and Integration	3			
Non-Functional Testing	3			
Peer Reviews	3			
Test Measurement	4	Objective maturity level 4		
Product Quality Evaluation	4			
Advanced Reviews	4			
Defect Prevention	5	Objective maturity level 5		
Test Process Optimization	5			
Quality Control	5			

3 TMMi Process Areas, Generic Goals and Practices

3.1 Introduction

This chapter describes the purposes of process areas, generic goals, generic practices, specific goals and specific practices of TMMi. The complete TMMi framework can be downloaded from the TMMi Foundation website (www.TMMifoundation.org) free of cost.

This chapter first presents the generic goals and practices, followed by the process areas with their purposes, their specific goals and their specific practices. The goals and practices have been numbered uniquely using GG for generic goal, GP for generic practice, SG for specific goal and SP for specific practice. While in this book the generic goals and practices are explained, the specific goals and practices are not. The motivation for adding an explanation of the generic goals and practices is twofold. First, one of the differences between TMMi and other test improvement models is the explicit attention that is paid to institutionalization thus guaranteeing that improvements do not only work temporarily, but become an integral part of the organization in the long term. Secondly, during the review process of this book it appeared that the TMMi audience needed more background and more explanation on these topics specifically.

The TMMi documentation describes the goals and practices in great detail. For example, for every practice a number of informative TMMi components have been clarified. Examples of these are typical work products and sub-practices. These components are not obligatory and need not be expected, but are included as a means of illustration. These informative TMMi components have not been added to this book because of their size, but are strongly recommended as background material.

The specific process areas, shown in Section 3.3, have been ordered according to maturity level.

3.2 Generic Goals and Practices

GG 2 Institutionalize a Managed Process

The process is institutionalized as a managed process.

A managed process is a process that accomplishes the work necessary to produce work products, is planned and executed in accordance with policy, utilizes skilled employees with adequate resources to produce controlled outputs, involves relevant stakeholders, is monitored, controlled and reviewed, and is evaluated for adherence to its process descriptions.

The process may be instantiated by a project, group, or organizational unit. The control provided by a managed process helps to ensure that the established process is retained during times of stress.

GP 2.1 Establish an organizational policy

Establish and maintain an organizational policy for planning and performing the process.

The purpose of this generic practice is to define the organizational expectations for the process and make these expectations visible to those in the organization who are affected. In general, senior management is responsible for establishing and communicating guiding principles, direction, and expectations for the organization.

GP 2.2 Plan the process

Establish and maintain the plan for performing the process.

The purpose of this generic practice is to determine what is needed to perform the process and to achieve the established objectives, to prepare a plan for performing the process, to prepare a process description, and to get agreement on the plan from relevant stakeholders by performing reviews.

GP 2.3 Provide resources

Provide adequate resources for performing the process, developing the test work products, and providing the services of the process.

The purpose of this generic practice is to ensure that resources necessary to perform the process as defined by the plan are available when they are needed. Resources include adequate funding, appropriate physical facilities, skilled people, and appropriate tools.

GP 2.4   Assign responsibilities

Assign responsibility and authority for performing the process, developing the work products, and providing the services of the process.

The purpose of this generic practice is to ensure that there is accountability for performing the process and achieving the specified results throughout the life of the process. The people assigned must have the appropriate authority to perform the assigned responsibilities. Responsibilities can be assigned using detailed job descriptions or in living documents, such as the plan for performing the process.

GP 2.5   Train people

Train the people performing or supporting the process as needed.

The purpose of this generic practice is to ensure that the people have the necessary skills and expertise to perform or support the process. Appropriate training is provided to the people who will perform the work. Overview training is provided to orient people who interact with those performing the work. Training supports the successful performance of the process by establishing a common understanding of the process, and by imparting the skills and knowledge needed to perform the process.

GP 2.6   Manage configuration

Place designated work products of the process under appropriate levels of configuration control.

The purpose of this generic practice is to establish and maintain the integrity of the designated work products of the process throughout their useful life. The designated work products are specifically identified in the plan for performing the process, along with a specification of the level of configuration management, e.g., version control or formal configuration management using baselines.

Examples of configuration management practices include version control, change history and control, status identification and usage of configuration management tools for storage. Refer to the Configuration Management process area within CMMI for more information on placing work products under configuration management.

GP 2.7   Identify and involve relevant stakeholders

Identify and involve relevant stakeholders of the process as planned.

The purpose of this generic practice is to establish and maintain the expected involvement of stakeholders during the execution of the process. Relevant stakeholders are involved in activities such as planning, making decisions, establishing commitments, communicating, conducting reviews and resolving problems. Critical stakeholders in the testing process include managers and users/customers.

The manager's role involves commitment and the ability to perform activities and tasks related to improving the testing capability. The user's or customer's role involves co-operating, providing support and sometimes actually performing testing activities. Users/customers should be involved in quality-related activities and tasks that concern user-oriented needs. The focus of this interaction is on soliciting user/customer support, reaching consensus and participating in activities such as product risk analysis, acceptance testing and possibly usability testing.

Depending on the test level, the developer may also be a stakeholder in the testing activities. For example, during component testing the developer often performs the testing activities himself but at the acceptance test level the developer is involved in discussing incidents found, agreeing on entry criteria, etc.

GP 2.8   Monitor and control the process

Monitor and control the process against the plan for performing the process and take appropriate actions.

The purpose of this generic practice is to perform the direct day-to-day monitoring and control of the test process. Adequate visibility into the test process is maintained so that appropriate corrective action can be taken when necessary. Monitoring and controlling the process involves measuring appropriate attributes of the test process and the work products produced by the test process. Refer to the Measurement and Analysis process area within CMMI for more information on measurement.

GP 2.9   Objectively evaluate adherence

Objective evaluate adherence of the process against its process description, standards, and procedures, and address non-compliances.

The purpose of this generic practice is to provide credible assurance that the process is implemented as planned and adheres to its process description, standard, and procedures. People not directly responsible for managing or performing the activities of a test process typically evaluate adherence. In many cases, adherence is evaluated by people within the organization, but external to the test process or project. Refer to the Process and Product Quality Assurance process area within CMMI for more information on objectively evaluating adherence.

GP 2.10   Review status with higher level management

Review the activities, status and results of the process with higher level management and resolve issues.

The purpose of this generic practice is to provide higher level management with the appropriate visibility into the process. Higher level management includes those levels of management in the organization above the immediate level of management responsible for performing the process. These reviews are for managers who provide policy and overall guidance for the process, not for those who perform the direct day-to-day monitoring and controlling of the process.

GG 3 Institutionalize a Defined Process

The process is institutionalized as a defined process.

A defined process is a managed process that is tailored from the organization's set of standard processes according to the organization's tailoring guidelines. A defined process has maintained process descriptions and contributes work products, measures, and other process improvement information to the organizational process assets.

A critical distinction between a managed process and a defined process is the scope of application of the process descriptions, standards, and procedures. For a managed process, descriptions, standards, and procedures are applicable to a particular project, group, or organizational function. As a result, the managed processes of two projects in one organization may be different. A defined process is standardized as much as possible across the organization and is adapted only when required for a specific project or organizational function based on the published tailoring guidelines.

GP 3.1   Establish a defined process

Establish and maintain a description of a defined process.

The purpose of this generic practice is to establish and maintain a description of any process that has been tailored to address the needs of a specific instantiation of the process. The organization should have standard processes that cover the process area, as well as guidelines for tailoring these standard processes to meet the needs of a project or organizational function. With a defined process, variability in how the processes are performed across the organization is reduced and process assets, data, and learning can be effectively shared. Refer to the Organization Process Definition process area within CMMI for more information about the organization's set of standard processes and tailoring guidelines.

GP 3.2   Collect improvement information

Collect work products, measures, measurement results, and improvement information derived from planning and performing the process to support the future use and improvement of the organization's processes and process assets.

The purpose of this generic practice is to collect information and artifacts derived from planning and performing the process to support future use and improvement of the organization's processes and process assets. The information and artifacts are stored and made available to those who are (or who will be) planning and performing the same or similar processes.

3.3 Specific Goals and Specific Practices

3.3.1 TMMi Level 2 Process Areas

PA 2.1 Test Policy and Strategy

The purpose of the Test Policy and Strategy process area is to develop and establish a test policy, and an organization-wide or program-wide test strategy in which the test levels are unambiguously defined. To measure test performance, test performance indicators are introduced.

SG 1 Establish a Test Policy

A test policy, aligned with the business (quality) policy, is established and agreed upon by the stakeholders.

SP 1.1 Define test goals

Define and maintain test goals based upon business needs and objectives.

SP 1.2 Define test policy

A test policy, aligned with the business (quality) policy, is defined based on the test goals and agreed upon by the stakeholders.

SP 1.3 Distribute the test policy to stakeholders

The test policy and test goals are presented and explained to stakeholders inside and outside testing.

SG 2 Establish a Test Strategy

An organization-wide or program-wide test strategy that identifies and defines the test levels to be performed, is established and deployed.

SP 2.1 Perform a generic product risk assessment

A generic product risk assessment is performed to identify the typical critical areas for testing.

SP 2.2 Define test strategy

The test strategy is defined that identifies and defines the test levels. For each level, the objectives, responsibilities, main tasks, entry/exit criteria and so forth are defined.

SP 2.3 Distribute the test strategy to stakeholders

The test strategy is presented to and discussed with stakeholders inside and outside testing.

SG 3 Establish Test Performance Indicators

A set of goal-oriented test process performance indicators to measure the quality of the test process is established and deployed.

SP 3.1 Define test performance indicators

The test performance indicators are defined based upon the test policy and goals, including a procedure for data collection, storage and analysis.

SP 3.2 Deploy test performance indicators

Deploy the test performance indicators and provide measurement results for the identified test performance indicators to stakeholders.

PA 2.2 Test Planning

The purpose of Test Planning is to define a test approach based on the identified risks and the defined test strategy, and to establish and maintain well-founded plans for performing and managing the testing activities.

SG 1 Perform a Product Risk Assessment

A product risk assessment is performed to identify the critical areas for testing.

SP 1.1 Define product risk categories and parameters

Product risk categories and parameters are defined that will be used during the product risk assessment.

SP 1.2 Identify product risks

Product risks are identified and documented.

SP 1.3 Analyze product risks

Product risks are evaluated, categorized and prioritized using the predefined product risk categories and parameters.

SG 2 Establish a Test Approach

A test approach, based on identified product risks, is established and agreed upon.

SP 2.1 Identify items and features to be tested

The items and features to be tested, and not to be tested, are identified based on the product risks.

SP 2.2 Define the test approach

The test approach is defined to mitigate the identified and prioritized product risks.

SP 2.3 Determine entry criteria

The entry criteria for testing are defined to prevent testing from starting under conditions that do not allow for a thorough test process.

SP 2.4 Determine exit criteria

The exit criteria for testing are defined to know determine when testing is complete.

SP 2.5 Determine suspension and resumption criteria

Criteria are defined that will be used to suspend and resume all or a portion of the test tasks on the test items and/or features.

SG 3 Establish Test Estimates

Well-founded test estimates are established and maintained for use in discussing the test approach with stakeholders and in planning the testing activities.

SP 3.1 Establish a top-level work breakdown structure

Establish a top-level work breakdown structure (WBS) to clearly define the scope of the testing to be performed and, thereby, the scope for the test estimate.

SP 3.2 Define test lifecycle

Define the test lifecycle phases on which to scope the planning effort.

SP 3.3 Determine estimates for test effort and cost

Estimate the test effort and cost for the test work products to be created and testing tasks to be performed based on the estimation rationale.

SG 4 Develop a Test Plan

A test plan is established and maintained as the basis for managing testing and communication to stakeholders.

SP 4.1 Establish the test schedule

The test schedule, with predefined stages of manageable size, is established and maintained based on the developed test estimate and defined test lifecycle.

SP 4.2 Plan for test staffing

A plan is created for the availability of the necessary test staff resources who have the required knowledge and skills to perform the testing.

SP 4.3 Plan stakeholder involvement

A plan is created for the involvement of the identified stakeholders.

SP 4.4 Identify test project risks

The test project risks associated with testing are identified, analyzed and documented.

SP 4.5 Establish the test plan

The test plan is established and maintained as a basis for managing testing and guiding the communication with the stakeholders.

SG 5 Obtain Commitment to the Test Plan

Commitments to the test plan are established and maintained.

SP 5.1 **Review test plan**

Review the test plan (and possibly other plans) that affect testing to achieve and understand test commitments.

SP 5.2 **Reconcile work and resource levels**

Review the test plan and update as necessary to reflect the available and estimated resources.

SP 5.3 **Obtain test plan commitments**

Obtain commitments from relevant stakeholders responsible for performing and supporting the execution of the test plan.

PA 2.3 Test Monitoring and Control

The purpose of Test Monitoring and Control is to provide an understanding of test progress and product quality so that appropriate corrective actions can be taken when test progress deviates significantly from plan or product quality deviates significantly from expectations.

SG 1 Monitor Test Progress against Plan

The actual progress and performance of testing is monitored against the test plan.

SP 1.1 **Monitor test planning parameters**

Monitor the actual values of the test planning parameters (e.g., test costs, lead time, hours and number of test cases) and compare against the values in the test plan.

SP 1.2 **Monitor test environment resources provided and used**

Monitor the test environment resources provided and used against those defined in the plan.

SP 1.3 **Monitor test commitments**

Monitor test commitments achieved against those identified in the test plan.

SP 1.4 **Monitor test project risks**

Monitor test project risks against those identified in the test plan.

SP 1.5 **Monitor stakeholder involvement**

Monitor stakeholder involvement against the expectations defined in the test plan.

SP 1.6 **Conduct test progress reviews**

Periodically review test progress, performance and issues.

SP 1.7 **Conduct test progress milestone reviews**

Review the accomplishments and progress of testing at selected test milestones.

SG 2 Monitor Product Quality against Plan and Expectations

Actual product quality is monitored against the quality measurements defined in the plan and the quality expectations, e.g., of the customer/user.

SP 2.1   Check against entry criteria

At the start of the test execution phase check the status against the entry criteria identified in the test plan.

SP 2.2   Monitor defects

Monitor measures of defects found during testing against expectations.

SP 2.3   Monitor product risks

Monitor product risks against those identified in the test plan.

SP 2.4   Monitor exit criteria

Monitor the status of the exit criteria against those identified in the test plan.

SP 2.5   Monitor suspension and resumption criteria

Monitor the status of the suspension and resumption criteria against those identified in the test plan.

SP 2.6   Conduct product quality reviews

Periodically review product quality.

SP 2.7   Conduct product quality milestone reviews

Review product quality status at selected test milestones.

SG 3 Manage Corrective Actions to Closure

Corrective actions are managed to closure when test progress or product quality deviate significantly from the test plan or expectations.

SP 3.1   Analyze issues

Collect and analyze the issues and determine the corrective actions necessary to address the issues.

SP 3.2   Take corrective action

Take corrective action as appropriate for the identified issues.

SP 3.3   Manage corrective action

Manage the corrective action to closure.

PA 2.4 Test Design and Execution

The purpose of Test Design and Execution is to improve the test process capability during test design and execution by establishing test design specifications, using test design techniques, performing a structured test execution process and managing test incidents to closure.

SG 1 Perform Test Analysis and Design using Test Design Techniques

During test analysis and design, the test approach is translated into tangible test conditions and test cases using test design techniques.

SP 1.1 Identify and prioritize test conditions

Test conditions are identified and prioritized using test design techniques, based on an analysis of the test items as specified in the test basis.

SP 1.2 Identify and prioritize test cases

Test cases are identified and prioritized using test design techniques.

SP 1.3 Identify necessary specific test data

Specific test data necessary to support the test conditions and execution of test cases is identified.

SP 1.4 Maintain horizontal traceability with requirements

Traceability between the requirements and the test conditions is established and maintained.

SG 2 Perform Test Implementation

During test implementation, the test procedures are developed and prioritized, including the intake test. Test data is created, and the test execution schedule is defined during this phase.

SP 2.1 Develop and prioritize test procedures

Test procedures are developed and prioritized.

SP 2.2 Create specific test data

Specific test data, as specified during the test analysis and design activity, is created.

SP 2.3 Specify intake test procedure

The intake test is specified. This test, sometimes called the confidence or smoke test is used to decide at the beginning of test execution whether the test object is ready for detailed and further testing.

SP 2.4 Develop test execution schedule

A test execution schedule is developed that describes the sequence in which the test procedures will be executed.

SG 3 Perform Test Execution

Tests are executed according to the previously specified test procedures and test schedule. Incidents are reported and test logs are written.

SP 3.1 **Perform intake test**

Perform the intake test (confidence test) to decide whether the test object is ready for detailed and further testing.

SP 3.2 **Execute test cases**

According to the defined execution schedule, the test cases are run either manually using documented test procedures and/or via test automation using pre-defined test scripts.

SP 3.3 **Report test incidents**

Discrepancies between the actual and expected results are reported as test incidents.

SP 3.4 **Write test log**

Test logs are written to provide a chronological record of relevant details about the execution of the tests.

SG 4 **Manage Test Incidents to Closure**

Test incidents are managed and resolved as appropriate.

SP 4.1 **Decide disposition of test incidents in configuration control board**

Appropriate actions on test incidents are decided upon by a configuration control board (CCB).

SP 4.2 **Perform appropriate action to close the test incident**

Appropriate actions are taken to fix, re-test and close the test incidents or defer the incident(s) to a future release.

SP 4.3 **Track the status of test incidents**

The status of the test incidents is tracked and appropriate actions are taken as needed.

PA 2.5 Test Environment

The purpose of Test Environment is to establish and maintain an adequate environment, including test data, in which it is possible to execute the tests in a manageable and repeatable way.

SG 1 **Develop Test Environment Requirements**

Stakeholder needs, expectations and constraints are collected and translated into test environment requirements.

SP 1.1 **Elicit test environment needs**

Elicit test environment, including generic test data, needs, expectations and constraints.

SP 1.2 **Develop the test environment requirements**

Transform the test environment needs into test environment requirements

SP 1.3   Analyze the test environment requirements

Analyze the requirements to ensure they are necessary, sufficient and feasible.

SG 2 Perform Test Environment Implementation

The test environment requirements are implemented and the test environment is made available to be used during test execution.

SP 2.1   Implement the test environment

Implement the test environment as specified in the test environment requirements specification and according to the defined plan.

SP 2.2   Create generic test data

Generic test data as specified in the requirements specification is created.

SP 2.3   Specify test environment intake test procedure

The test environment intake test (confidence test), to be used to decide whether the test environment is ready for testing, is specified.

SP 2.4   Perform test environment intake test

The test environment intake test (confidence test) is performed to determine whether the test environment is ready to be used for testing.

SG 3 Manage and Control Test Environments

Test environments are managed and controlled to allow for uninterrupted test execution.

SP 3.1   Perform systems management

Systems management is performed on the test environments to effectively and efficiently support the test execution process.

SP 3.2   Perform test data management

Test data is managed and controlled to effectively and efficiently support the test execution process.

SP 3.3   Coordinate the availability and usage of the test environments

The availability and usage of the test environment by multiple groups is coordinated to achieve maximum efficiency.

SP 3.4   Report and manage test environment incidents

Problems that occur when using the test environment are formally reported as incidents and are managed to closure.

3.3.2 TMMi Level 3 Process Areas

PA 3.1 Test Organization

The purpose of the Test Organization process area is to identify and organize a group of highly skilled people that is responsible for testing. In addition to testing, the test group also manages improvements to the organization's test process and test process assets based on a thorough understanding of the strengths and weaknesses of the organization's current test process and test process assets.

SG 1 Establish a Test Organization

A test organization, which supports the testing practices in projects and the organization, is defined and established.

SP 1.1   Define the test organization

A test organization is defined and agreed upon by the stakeholders.

SP 1.2   Obtain commitments for the test organization

Commitments for implementing and supporting the test organization are established and maintained.

SP 1.3   Implement the test organization

The test organization is implemented in the organization, based on the committed test organization definition.

SG 2 Establish Test Functions for Test Specialists

Test functions with accompanying job descriptions are established and assigned to the test specialists.

SP 2.1   Identify test functions

A set of test functions is identified, as appropriate.

SP 2.2   Develop job descriptions

For the test functions identified, job descriptions are developed. For non-test specialist functions, existing job descriptions are enhanced with typical test tasks and responsibilities, as appropriate.

SP 2.3   Assign staff members to test functions

Members of the test organization are assigned to the identified test functions.

SG 3 Establish Test Career Paths

Test career paths are established that allow testers to improve their knowledge, skills, status and rewards.

SP 3.1   Establish test career paths

Test career paths are defined that will allow testers to advance their careers.

SP 3.2   Develop personal test career development plans

A personal test career development plan is developed and maintained for every member of the test organization.

SG 4   Determine, Plan and Implement Test Process Improvements

Strengths, weaknesses, and improvement opportunities for the organization's test process are identified periodically and as needed. Process changes that address the improvements are planned and implemented.

SP 4.1   Assess the organization's test process

The organization's test process periodically is assessed to maintain an understanding of its strengths and weaknesses.

SP 4.2   Identify the organization's test process improvements

Desirable improvements to the organization's test process and test process assets are identified.

SP 4.3   Plan test process improvements

Actions that are needed to address improvements to the organization's test process and test process assets are planned.

SP 4.4   Implement test process improvements

The test process improvements addressed by the test improvement plan are implemented.

SG 5   Deploy the Organizational Test Process and Incorporate Lessons Learned

The organizational standard test process and test process assets are deployed across the organization and test process-related experiences are incorporated into the organizational test process and test process assets.

SP 5.1   Deploy standard test process and test process assets

The standard test process and test process assets are deployed across the organization, especially to projects at their startup, and changes are deployed as appropriate throughout the life of each project.

SP 5.2   Monitor implementation

The implementation of the organization's standard test process and the use of the test process assets on projects is monitored.

SP 5.3   **Incorporate lessons learned into the organizational test process**

Lessons learned from planning and performing the test process are incorporated into the organizational standard test process and test process assets.

PA 3.2 Test Training Program

The purpose of the Test Training Program process area is to develop a training program which facilitates the development of the knowledge and skills of people so that test tasks and roles can be performed effectively and efficiently.

SG 1   Establish an Organizational Test Training Capability

A training capability, which supports the organization's test roles, is established and maintained.

SP 1.1   **Identify the strategic test training needs**

The strategic test training needs of the organization are identified and maintained.

SP 1.2   **Align the organizational and project test training needs**

The organizational and project test training needs are aligned and it is determined which of the test training needs are the responsibility of the organization and which should be left to the individual projects.

SP 1.3   **Establish an organizational test training plan**

An organizational test training plan is established and maintained.

SP 1.4   **Establish test training capability**

A test training capability is established and maintained to address the organizational training needs and to support the project-specific training needs.

SG 2   Provide Necessary Test Training

Training necessary to perform their role effectively is provided for testers and other individuals involved in testing.

SP 2.1   **Deliver test training**

Training is delivered according to the organizational test training plan.

SP 2.2   **Establish test training records**

Records showing the organizational test training that has been conducted are created and maintained.

SP 2.3   Assess test training effectiveness

The effectiveness of the organization's test training program is assessed.

PA 3.3 Test Lifecycle and Integration

The purpose of Test Lifecycle and Integration is to establish and maintain a usable set of organizational test process assets (e.g., a standard test lifecycle) and work environment standards and to integrate and synchronize the test lifecycle with the development lifecycle. The integrated lifecycle ensures early involvement of testing in a project. The purpose of Test Lifecycle and Integration is also to define a coherent test approach across multiple test levels, based on the identified risks and the defined test strategy, and to provide an overall test plan, based on the defined test lifecycle.

SG 1 Establish Organizational Test Process Assets

A set of organizational test process assets is established and maintained.

SP 1.1   Establish standard test processes

The organization's set of standard test processes is established and maintained.

SP 1.2   Establish test lifecycle model descriptions addressing all test levels

Descriptions of the test lifecycle models (including supporting templates and guidelines for the test deliverables) that are approved for use in the organization are established and maintained, ensuring coverage of all identified test levels.

SP 1.3   Establish tailoring criteria and guidelines

The tailoring criteria and guidelines for the organization's set of standard test processes are established and maintained.

SP 1.4   Establish the organization's test process database

The organization's test process database is established and maintained.

SP 1.5   Establish the organization's test process asset library

The organization's test process asset library is established and maintained.

SP 1.6   Establish work environment standards

The work environment standards are established and maintained.

SG 2   Integrate the Test Lifecycle Models with the Development Models

The test lifecycle is integrated, ensuring early test involvement, with the development lifecycle in terms of phasing, milestones, deliverables and activities.

SP 2.1   Establish integrated lifecycle models

Descriptions of the integrated test and development lifecycle models that are approved for use in the organization are established and maintained.

SP 2.2   Review integrated lifecycle models

The integrated lifecycle models are reviewed with the stakeholders to promote their understanding of the role of testing within the integrated test and development lifecycle models.

SP 2.3   Obtain commitments on the role of testing within the integrated lifecycle models

Commitments are obtained regarding the role of testing within the integrated lifecycle models from the relevant stakeholders who are responsible for managing, performing and supporting project activities based on the integrated lifecycle models.

SG 3   Establish a Master Test Plan

A master test plan is established to define a coherent test approach across multiple test levels and an overall test planning.

SP 3.1   Perform product risk assessment

A product risk assessment is performed to identify the typical critical areas for testing.

SP 3.2   Establish the test approach

The test approach is established and agreed upon to mitigate the identified and prioritized product risks.

SP 3.3   Establish test estimates

Well-founded test estimates are established and maintained for use in discussing the test approach with stakeholders and in planning the testing activities.

SP 3.4   Define the organization for testing

The organization of the testing at the various levels is defined, including the interfaces to other processes, and a clear overview of what is expected from the various parties involved is established.

SP 3.5   Develop the master test plan

The master test plan is established to define a coherent test approach across multiple test levels.

SP 3.6   Obtain commitment to the master test plan

Commitments to the master test plan are established and maintained.

PA 3.4 Non-Functional Testing

The purpose of the Non-Functional Testing process area is to improve test process capability to include non-functional testing during test planning, test design and execution. This is done by defining a test approach based on the identified non-functional product risks, establishing non-functional test specifications and executing a structured test execution process focused on non-functional testing.

SG 1   Perform a Non-Functional Product Risk Assessment

A product risk assessment is performed to identify the critical areas for non-functional testing.

SP 1.1   Identify non-functional product risks

Non-functional product risks are identified and documented.

SP 1.2   Analyze non-functional product risks

Non-functional product risks are evaluated, categorized and prioritized using predefined categories and parameters.

SG 2   Establish a Non-Functional Test Approach

A test approach for non-functional testing, based on identified non-functional product risks, is established and agreed upon.

SP 2.1   Identify features to be tested

The non-functional features to be tested, and not to be tested, are identified based on the non-functional product risks.

SP 2.2   Define the non-functional test approach

The test approach is defined to mitigate the identified and prioritized non-functional product risks.

SP 2.3   Define non-functional exit criteria

The exit criteria for non-functional testing are defined to plan when to stop testing.

SG 3   Perform Non-Functional Test Analysis and Design

During test analysis and design the test approach for non-functional testing is translated into tangible test conditions and test cases.

SP 3.1   Identify and prioritize non-functional test conditions

Test conditions are identified and prioritized, based on an analysis of the non-functional features as specified in the test basis.

SP 3.2   Identify and prioritize non-functional test cases

Non-functional test cases are identified and prioritized to address the defined test conditions.

SP 3.3   Identify necessary specific test data

Specific test data necessary to support the non-functional test conditions and test cases is identified.

SP 3.4   Maintain horizontal traceability with non-functional require-ments

Maintain horizontal traceability from non-functional requirements to non-functional test conditions.

SG 4   Perform Non-Functional Test Implementation

Non-functional test procedures are developed and prioritized, and specific test data required for non-functional testing is created.

SP 4.1   Develop and prioritize non-functional test procedures

Non-functional test procedures are developed and priori-tized.

SP 4.2   Create specific test data

Specific test data to support the non-functional testing as specified during the test analysis and design activity is cre-ated.

SG 5   Perform Non-Functional Test Execution

Non-functional tests are executed according to previously specified test procedures. Incidents are reported and test logs are written.

SP 5.1   Execute non-functional test cases

The non-functional test cases are executed manually using documented test procedures and/or automatically using test scripts.

SP 5.2   Report non-functional test incidents

Differences between actual and expected results are reported as non-functional test incidents.

SP 5.3   Write test log

Test logs are written to provide a chronological record of relevant details about the execution of the non-functional tests.

PA 3.5 Peer Reviews

The purpose of the Peer Review process area is to verify that work products meet their specified requirements and to remove defects from selected work products early and efficiently. An important corollary effect is to develop a better understanding of the work products and of defects that might be prevented.

SG 1 Establish a Peer Review Approach

A review approach is established and agreed upon.

SP 1.1 Identify work products to be reviewed

The work products to be reviewed are identified, including the type of review and critical participants (stakeholders) to involve.

SP 1.2 Define peer review criteria

Preparation for peer reviews on selected work products is accomplished by defining and maintaining entry and exit criteria for peer reviews.

SG 2 Perform Peer Reviews

Peer reviews are performed on selected work products and peer review data is analyzed.

SP 2.1 Conduct peer reviews

Selected work products are peer reviewed and issues are identified.

SP 2.2 Testers review test basis documents

The documents that are used as a basis for testing are reviewed by the testers.

SP 2.3 Analyze peer review data

The peer review data regarding preparation, conduct, and results of the reviews is analyzed.

3.3.3 TMMi Level 4 Process Areas

PA 4.1 Test Measurement

The purpose of Test Measurement is to identify, collect, analyze and apply measurements to support an organization in objectively evaluating the effectiveness and efficiency of the test process, the productivity of its testing staff, the resulting product quality and the results of test improvement. As such, the test organization will develop and sustain a test measurement capability that is used to support management information needs.

SG 1 Align Test Measurement and Analysis Activities

Test measurement objectives and activities are aligned with identified information needs and objectives.

SP 1.1   Establish test measurement objectives

Test measurement objectives that are derived from identified information needs and business objectives are established and maintained.

SP 1.2   Specify test measures

The test measures are specified that will address the test measurement objectives.

SP 1.3   Specify data collection and storage procedures

Collection methods are explicitly specified to ensure that the right data are collected properly. Storage and retrieval procedures are specified to ensure that data are available and accessible for future use.

SP 1.4   Specify analysis procedures

Data analysis procedures are specified in advance to ensure that appropriate analysis will be conducted and reliable test measurement data is reported to address the documented test measurement objectives (and thereby the information needs and objectives on which they are based).

SG 2 Provide Test Measurement Results

Test measurement results that address information needs and objectives are provided.

SP 2.1   Collect test measurement data

The test measurement data necessary for analysis are obtained and checked for completeness and integrity.

SP 2.2   Analyze test measurement data

The collected test measurement data are analyzed as planned and additional analysis is conducted as necessary.

SP 2.3   Communicate results

Results of test measurement activities are communicated to all relevant stakeholders.

SP 2.4   Store data and results

The test measurement data, measurement specification and analysis results are stored and managed.

PA 4.2 Product Quality Evaluation

The purpose of Product Quality Evaluation is to develop a quantitative understanding of the quality of the products and thereby support the achievement of specific projects' product quality goals.

SG 1   Measurable Project Goals for Product Quality and their Priorities are Established

A set of measurable and prioritized project goals for product quality is established and maintained.

SP 1.1   Identify product quality needs

Project product quality needs are identified and prioritized.

SP 1.2   Define the project's quantitative product quality goals

The project's quantitative product quality goals are defined based on the project's product quality needs.

SP 1.3   Define the approach for measuring progress toward the project's product quality goals

The approach is defined for measuring the level of accomplishment toward the defined set of product quality goals.

SG 2   Actual Progress toward Achieving the Project's Product Quality Goals is Quantified and Managed

The project is monitored to determine whether the project's product quality goals will be satisfied, and to identify corrective action as appropriate.

SP 2.1   Measure product quality quantitatively throughout the lifecycle

The quality of the product and work products delivered by the project are quantitatively measured throughout the lifecycle based on the defined approach.

SP 2.2   Analyze product quality measurements and compare them to the product's quantitative goals

The (interim) product quality measurements are analyzed and compared to the project's (interim) product quality goals on an event-driven and periodic basis.

PA 4.3 Advanced Reviews

The purpose of Advanced Reviews, building on the practices of the TMMi level 3 process area Peer Reviews, is to measure product quality early in the lifecycle and to enhance the test strategy and test approach by aligning peer reviews (static testing) with dynamic testing.

SG 1 Coordinate the Peer Review Approach with the Dynamic Test Approach

The approach for peer reviews (static testing) is aligned and coordinated with the approach for dynamic testing.

SP 1.1 Relate work products to items and features to be tested

For the item and features to be tested, as identified by the test approach, the related work products are identified.

SP 1.2 Define a coordinated test approach

A test approach is defined that coordinates both static and dynamic testing.

SG 2 Measure Product Quality Early in the Lifecycle by Means of Peer Reviews

Early in the lifecycle, product quality is measured against set criteria by means of peer reviews.

SP 2.1 Define peer review measurement guidelines

Guidelines to support the peer reviews as a measurement practice are defined and documented.

SP 2.2 Define peer review criteria based on product quality goals

Peer review criteria, especially quantitative exit criteria, are defined based on the project's (interim) product quality goals.

SP 2.3 Measure work product quality using peer reviews

The quality of the work products is measured early in the life cycle using peer reviews.

SG 3 Adjust the Test Approach Based on Review Results Early in the Lifecycle

Based on results of peer reviews early in the lifecycle, the test approach is adjusted as appropriate.

SP 3.1 Analyze peer review results

The collected peer review measurement data on work product quality are analyzed as planned.

SP 3.2 Revise the products risks as appropriate

Based on the peer review measurement data on work product quality, product risks are re-evaluated and re-prioritized using predefined categories and parameters.

SP 3.3 Revise the test approach as appropriate

The coordinated test approach, based on identified product risks, is revised as appropriate and agreed upon.

3.3.4 TMMi Level 5 Process Areas

PA 5.1 Defect Prevention

The purpose of Defect Prevention is to identify and analyze common causes of defects across the development lifecycle and define actions to prevent similar defects from occurring in the future.

SG1 Determine Common Causes of Defects

Root and common causes of selected defects are systematically determined.

SG2 Prioritize and Define Actions to Systematically Eliminate Root Causes of Defects

Actions are defined to systematically address root and common causes of defects to prevent their future occurrence.

PA 5.2 Quality Control

The purpose of Quality Control is to statistically manage and control the test process. Test process performance is fully predictable and stabilized with acceptable limits. Testing at a project level is performed using statistical methods based on representative samples in order to predict product quality and make testing more efficient.

SG1 Establish a Statistically Controlled Test Process

A statistically controlled test process is established whereby baselines and models that characterize the expected test process performance of the organization's standard test processes are established and maintained.

SG2 Testing is Performed using Statistical Methods

Tests are designed and executed using statistical methods (e.g., sampling, fault seeding) based on operational or usage profiles.

PA 5.3 Test Process Optimization

The purpose of Test Process Optimization is to continuously improve the existing testing processes used in the organization and to identify new testing technologies (e.g., test tools or test methods) that may be appropriate and to transition them into the organization in an orderly manner. Test process improvement also supports the re-use of test assets across the organization. The improvements support the organization's quality and process performance objectives as derived from the organization's business objectives.

SG1 Select Test Process Improvements

Test process improvements are selected which contribute to meeting product quality and test process-performance objectives.

SG2 New Testing Technologies are Evaluated to Determine their Impact on the Testing Process

New testing technologies such as tools, methods, techniques or technical innovations are identified, selected and evaluated to determine their effect on the organization's standard test process.

SG3 Deploy Test Improvements

Test process improvements and appropriate new technologies are deployed across the organization to improve the testing process. Their benefit is measured and information about new innovations is disseminated across the organization.

SG4 Establish Re-use of High Quality Test Assets

Both test process components and testware are recognized as assets and re-used across the organization when creating another test asset.

4 TMMi Assessments

4.1 Introduction

In a TMMi assessment the maturity of test processes is measured. An assessment can also determine if an organization has achieved a certain test maturity level or not. The results of the assessment can be used to formulate recommendations for improvement. The assessment results and recommendations help to determine action plans to implement improvements in test processes.

TMMi assessments can be executed at various moments. For example, a test process improvement program can start with an assessment to find the areas that need to be improved. During an improvement program, a TMMi assessment can be used to determine which accomplishments have been made so far. When an organization thinks a certain TMMi maturity level has been reached, this can be proven by a lead assessor conducting a formal assessment.

The TMMi Assessment Method Application Requirements (TAMAR) have been developed to execute assessments. TAMAR is not a defined assessment approach, but describes the requirements that TMMi assessments must meet. Organizations should develop their own assessment approach that is appropriate for their business; when this approach meets TAMAR, it can be officially accredited by the TMMi Foundation.

This chapter describes the different assessment types recognized by TAMAR. An example is provided that shows a TMMi assessment approach based on TAMAR. Finally, the certification process for TMMi assessors is described. A complete description of TAMAR can be found on the website of the TMMi Foundation (www.TMMifoundation.org).

4.2 Assessment Types

There are two assessment types: formal and informal. A formal assessment has enough depth to officially determine to what extent an organization meets the requirements as defined in TMMi. An informal assessment does not lead to an official result about the process maturity; it only provides an indication. An informal assessment is often used to identify the major improvements that need to be made and it can also be used determine the progress of a TMMi implementation. An informal assessment is often adequate as an initial survey, although a formal assessment can also be used for this.

Deciding which of the two assessment types is best depends on the requirements and expectations an organization has about the assessment. An example of the use of the two assessment types plotted against time is shown in Figure 4.1.

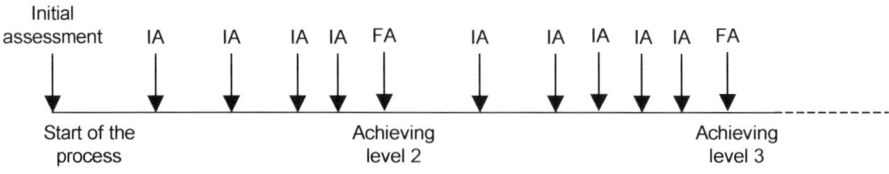

Figure 4.1: Assessment types plotted against time

In a formal assessment all the criteria of Table 4.1 must be met. In an informal assessment only the criteria of Table 4.2 must be met.

Table 4.1 Criteria of formal assessments			
Assessment team lead	**Assessment team size**	**Evidence collected**	**Capability Rating**
Accredited lead assessor	At least 2 (accredited lead assessor and at least 1 accredited assessor)	Staff interviews and document study required. Other types of evidence, such as questionnaires are recommended.	Verifiable benchmark rating of the organization against TMMi is produced; strengths and weaknesses identified in fine detail, including a full gap analysis

Table 4.2 Criteria of informal assessments			
Assessment Team Lead	**Assessment Team Size**	**Evidence collected**	**Capability Rating**
Experienced assessor	At least 1 person	One type of evidence (interviews, document study or questionnaires) is required	No rating against TMMi is produced. Utilized purely for 'quick check' assessments to gain a rough understanding of an organizational area's maturity level and improvements opportunities.

When a formal assessment is conducted, the requirements of an informal assessment are automatically met as well. When an assessment is conducted at a higher maturity level, the process areas at lower maturity levels are also assessed.

As can be seen in Tables 4.1 and 4.2, several different types of evidence can be collected. TAMAR uses the following types of evidence:
- Staff interviews
- Document study
- Questionnaires
- Customer surveys.

Formal Assessments
Formal assessments must be led by an accredited lead assessor. Lead assessor accreditation can only be achieved through the TMMi Foundation. For a formal assessment the assessment team must consist of a lead assessor and at least one other accredited assessor. Additional assessment team members need not be accredited.

Formal assessments require a strict level of evidence for the achievement of specific and generic goals of the relevant TMMi process areas. Evidence from multiple sources is needed to conduct a formal assessment. For a formal assessment it is mandatory for the assessment team to conduct staff interviews as one point of evidence. The data collected from the interviews must to be corroborated with the findings from the document study. Data for a formal assessment can also be collected from other sources, such as questionnaires and customer surveys. The data must be collected from different sources and different parts of the organization to determine whether a TMMi practice has been institutionalized.

One of the results of a formal assessment is a full gap analysis showing the strengths and weaknesses of an organization against the TMMi model. This gap analysis can be used as the basis for future improvement projects.

Informal Assessments
Informal assessments are conducted with less rigor than is required by formal assessments and are, therefore, faster and cheaper, but are also less precise. Informal assessments are designed as an initial indicative view and 'quick check' to evaluate the current state of the test processes against TMMi. Informal assessments are led by an experienced assessor, who need not be formally accredited although this is highly recommended.

An assessment team for an informal assessment can consist of a single person. This corresponds with the aim of informal assessments being quick, low-impact evaluations that may result in less accurate outcomes. To draw conclusions in an informal assessment only one type of evidence needs to be supplied, any type of evidence is accepted and no formal corroboration of the evidence is needed.

4.3 TMMi Assessment Method

This chapter discusses the TMMi assessment method in more detail.

Formal assessments need to be conducted using a fully documented and TAMAR accredited method. An example is provided of a typical formal TMMi assessment method.

A formal TMMi assessment typically acknowledges the following phases:
1. Planning phase
2. Preparation phase
3. Interview phase
4. Reporting phase

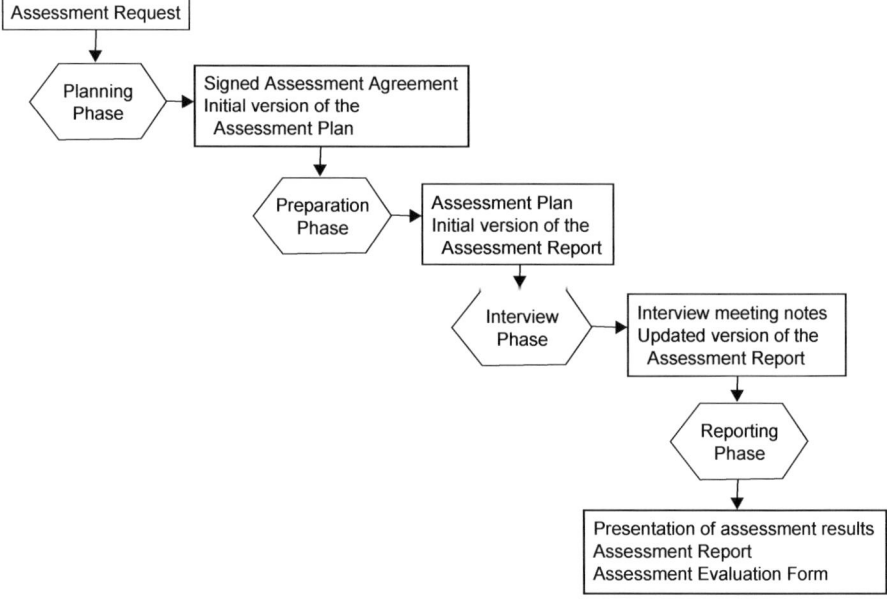

Figure 4.2: Example TMMi assessment phases [ITAM]

The different phases of a TMMi assessment are explained hereafter:

4.3.1 Planning Phase

The purpose of the planning phase is to come to an agreement with the Sponsor about the scope, costs, activities to be carried out, timeline, planned feedback sessions and reports.

The planning is executed using the assessment request (the documented or undocumented request of the client organization to conduct an assessment) and several conversations between the client and the (intended) assessor. Prior to its initiation, a plan for the assessment is formulated. This plan is distributed to all key stakeholders, among which are the Assessment Sponsor and the assessment team.

There are three main inputs to the assessment plan as follows:
1. The purpose of the assessment - for example, determining if a particular TMMi level has been attained, determining the defects in certain process areas or identifying TMMi recommendations for optimizing the test process.
2. The scope of the assessment - defines how wide-ranging the assessment is, including organizational elements, process areas and projects that will be covered.
3. The constraints - for example, availability of key resources, the maximum duration of the assessment, specific organizational areas to be excluded from the assessment and any confidentiality agreements that need to be taken into account.

The assessment plan identifies the activities, resources, schedules, responsibilities and includes a description of the intended assessment outputs. There are three defined roles within an assessment, the first of which is the assessment sponsor. The assessment sponsor is a person who is internal to the organization which is being assessed. He provides the necessary resources and impetus for the assessment to take place. The second role is that of assessment team leader. The assessment team leader organizes and coordinates all aspects of the assessment and ensures that the assessment team fulfils all objectives laid out for it throughout the course of the assessment. The third role is that of assessment team member. The assessment team member, or members, conduct the assessment and, together with the assessment team leader, evaluate the process areas using the evidence collected.

4.3.2 Preparation Phase

The purpose of the preparation phase is to prepare everything needed to conduct the assessment and to make a detailed schedule for the (optional) kick-off meeting, interviews, progress report, feedback sessions, presentation and report.

During this phase a document study is conducted. The document study starts with providing the organization with a checklist, in which the needed test documentation can be found. When the assessment team has been provided with this documentation, it can start the document study and thus present the current situation within the organization. The findings are documented in the initial version of the assessment report. It is important that when documenting the findings, the source of these documents is also recorded, so the results of the assessment can be verified.

4.3.3 Interview Phase

The purpose of the interview phase is to collect information about the current test practices. The activities that need to be executed are:
- Conducting interviews as a means to gather and verify information
- Performing a preliminary analysis, which can lead to additional questions in successive interviews or even to the planning of additional interviews

4.3.4 Reporting Phase

The purpose of the reporting phase is to give the organization feedback about the preliminary assessment findings thereby also validating the findings. After the validation of the findings, the assessment findings are made final. A second purpose of the reporting phase is to write and present the final report. The following activities are executed:
- Performing the analysis and determining the scores, including determining the TMMi level
- Formulating recommendations for follow-up activities
- Formulating the (preliminary) report and/or presentation
- Presenting the assessment results and recommendations.

An assessment report must contain the following items:
1. The time period in which the assessment was conducted
2. A list of inputs (documents, interview reports) that was used during the assessment
3. The findings ("the evidence") that were collected during the document study and the interviews
4. An overview of the assessment method that was used to conduct the assessment
5. Formal assessments give an overall TMMi classification as well. In informal assessments this is not possible.

Process Attribute Rating

During the assessment, the evidence is validated to determine whether the evidence is correct or not. To be able to draw conclusions a sufficient amount of evidence is needed and that evidence must be of sufficient depth. Whether the amount and depth of evidence is sufficient depends on the goal of the assessment.

The objective evidence is used to determine to what extent a certain goal has been reached. To be able to classify a specific or a generic goal, the classification of the underlying specific and generic practices needs to be determined. A process area as a whole is classified in accordance with the lowest classified goal that is met. The maturity level is determined in accordance with the lowest classified process area within that maturity level.

The level to which an organization achieves a particular process area is measured using a scale which consists of the following levels:
- N – Not achieved
- P – Partially achieved
- L – Largely achieved
- F – Fully achieved

To score "N" (Not Achieved), there should be little or no evidence found of compliance with the goals of the process area. The percentage of process achievement which would score "N" would be any score in the range from 0% to 15%. To score "P" (Partially Achieved) there should be some evidence found of compliance, but the process may be incomplete, not widespread, or inconsistently applied. The percentage of process achievement for processes which would score "P" would be any score over 15% and up to 50%. To score "L" (Largely Achieved) there should be significant evidence found of compliance, but there may still be some minor weaknesses in implementation, application or results of this process. The percentage of process achievement for processes which would score "L" would be any score over 50% and up to 85%. To score "F" (Fully Achieved) there should be consistent evidence found of compliance. The process has been implemented both systematically and completely and there should be no obvious weaknesses in implementation, application or results of this process. The percentage of process achievement for processes which would score "F" would be any score over 85% and up to 100%.

There are two additional ratings that can be utilized. These are:
- "Not Applicable", this classification is used if a process attribute is not applicable to the organization and is therefore excluded from the results;
- "Not Rated", this classification is used if the process attribute is not rateable due to insufficient evidence.

The attribute ratings must be traceable to the evidence. The rating given to an organization must be substantiated by the particular evidence that was found. Therefore the evidence, as well as the traceability between evidence and conclusions, must be recorded.

4.4 Certifying TMMi Assessors

The TMMi Foundation accredits assessors, the consultants conducting the assessments, on the basis of the accredited TMMi assessment method used by the assessor. This can be an assessment method developed by the organization in which the assessor is working or an assessment method licensed by another organization but used by the organization in which the assessor is working.

Candidates are accredited according to the experience they have. The criteria used for this are shown in Table 4.3.

Table 4.3 Assessor Accreditation Criteria		
Area of expertise	**Lead assessor** (formal assessments)	**Assessor** (informal assessments)
Testing	A minimum of five years of experience in different kinds of testing and in different types of organizations. Must be ISTQB Advanced certified.	A minimum of five years of experience in different kinds of testing and in different types of organizations. Must be ISTQB Foundation certified.
Test process improvement	A minimum of two years of experience, in which two years of experience in software process improvement equals one year of experience in test process improvement.	A minimum of one year of experience, in which two years of experience in software process improvement equals one year of experience in test process improvement.
TMMi	Attended TMMi training and has experience using TMMi.	Attended TMMi training and has experience using TMMi.
Assessments	Attended Assessment training and has 20 days of assessment experience	Attended Assessment training and has 10 days of assessment experience

An up-to-date list of accredited assessors is published on the TMMi Foundation website (www.TMMifoundation.org).

5 Implementing TMMi

5.1 Introduction

Primarily, TMMi is a list of best practices or a description of a mature test process. TMMi does not offer a standard approach to a change program in an organization. To support the implementation of models such as CMMI, the Software Engineering Institute (SEI) has developed a model for change processes: IDEAL [IDEAL]. This model has also proved to be very useful when implementing TMMi. IDEAL offers an extensive and practical reference standard for change processes and also shows what needs to be done when implementing TMMi improvements in an organization. The model contains a five phase improvement cycle as shown below:

Table 5.1 IDEAL five phase improvement cycle		
Acronym	**Phase**	**Goal**
I	Initiating	Establishing the initial improvement infrastructure for a successful improvement process.
D	Diagnosing	Determining the organization's current state as opposed to what it wants to achieve.
E	Establishing	Planning and specifying how the chosen situation will be established.
A	Acting	Executing the plan.
L	Learning	Learning by experience and improving the abilities to implement changes.

Organizations are free to choose the improvement approach for the implementation of TMMi. In addition to IDEAL, there are several other models for the implementation of process improvement. In general these models are based on Edward Deming's plan-do-check-act cycle. The Deming cycle starts with making a plan that determines the improvement goals and how they will be achieved (plan). Then the improvements are implemented (do) and it is determined whether the planned advantages have been achieved (check). Based on the results of this assessment further actions are taken as needed (act).

This chapter is about the phases and activities of IDEAL and the critical success factors of test improvement programs.

5.2 The Change Program

The phases of an improvement program in accordance with IDEAL are shown in Figure 5.1.

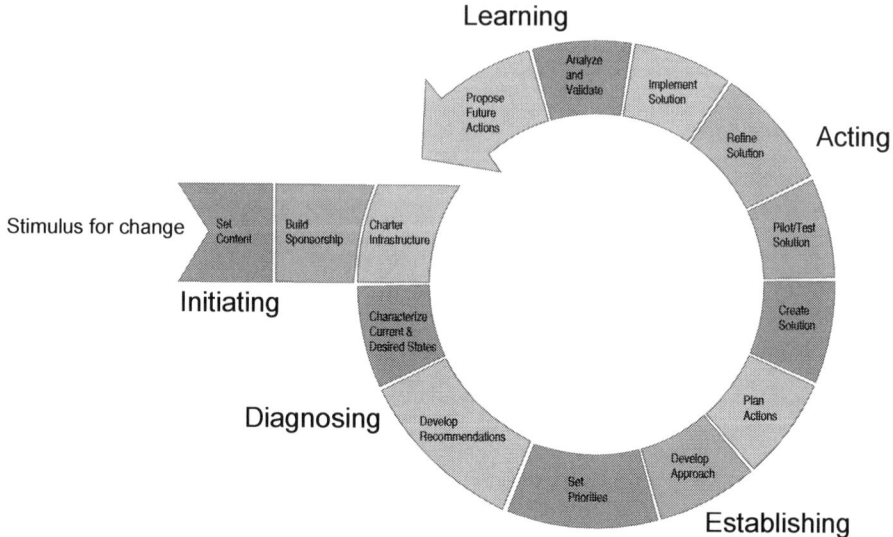

Figure 5.1: Phases of an improvement program in accordance with IDEAL [IDEAL]

The phases and activities are shortly described below.

5.2.1 I – Initiating: The Initiating Phase

In the Initiating phase the infrastructure for a successful change program is established. The goals and expected results with respect to the change and what needs to be contributed by the different parties concerned are defined. The goals of a TMMi implementation need to be in line with the quality goals and the organizational goals. In this phase the goals cannot always be formulated in a SMART (Specific, Measureable, Achievable, Realistic and Time-based) way, which is why the goals are specified in more detail in the Establishing phase. In this phase, management commitment requires explicit attention; management commitment is needed from test management, ICT management and business management. The Initiating phase has the following activities:
- Identify Stimulus for Change
- Set Context
- Build Sponsorship
- Charter Infrastructure.

Identify Stimulus for Change

Before the actual change project is started, the organization needs to realize that change is necessary. This can be stimulated for example by dissatisfaction with the results of current testing, unexpected incidents, changing circumstances, a senior management initiative, a benchmark result, a TMMi assessment, customer demand, market trends or information taken from an internal measurement repository. The proposed change needs to contribute to the success of the organization and needs to complement the existing quality and organizational goals. The extent to which the change is in accordance with the organizational goals largely determines the success of the change.

Set Context

The management needs to determine how the change effort fits the quality and business strategy. Which specific organizational goals will be realized or supported by the TMMi implementation? How are current projects influenced by the improvement? Which proceeds need to be yielded, for example in terms of fewer issues and incidents or the shortening of the lead time for test execution? During the project the context and effects will become more concrete, but it is important to be as clear as possible early in the project.

Build Sponsorship

Gaining support from the responsible managers, or building sponsorship, is extremely important in improvement projects. This concerns test management, IT management and business management sponsorship, because all these stakeholders will be influenced by the change. Sponsorship is important during the entire project, but because of the insecurity caused by changes, especially active support at the beginning of the project is important. Supporting the improvement program is an important part of sponsorship, but sponsorship is more, for example, providing active participation or promoting the project when there is resistance.

Charter Infrastructure

As a final activity in the Initiating phase, the way in which a change project is executed is determined. An infrastructure is put in place for this. The infrastructure must be described explicitly, including responsibilities and qualifications.

Usually the infrastructure consists of a project board guiding several improvement teams. In the project board are the sponsor, possibly the other sponsors of other improvement projects, the manager of the improvement program and possibly an external consultant. In addition there is often also an (external) TMMi expert. The project board is ultimately responsible for the improvement program and agrees on plans, milestones and final results. The project board has the ultimate power to decide and is the highest escalation level.

5.2.2 D – Diagnosing: The Diagnosing Phase

In the Diagnosing phase it is determined where the organization stands as opposed to what it wants to achieve. In order to do this, assessments are conducted in which measurements are compared to a reference standard, for example TMMi level 2. The current state of the organization is determined and its desired future state is clearly formulated. In the Diagnosing phase are the following activities:

- Characterize Current and Desired States
- Develop Recommendations.

Characterize Current and Desired States

TMMi can be used to define the desired state. An assessment, either formal or informal, is conducted to determine the current state (Chapter 4). The assessment may use the purposes and practices as a checklist to determine the maturity levels of the test processes. The desired state must align with the stimulus for change as determined in the initiating Phase and it must be within the realm of possibility for the organization.

Develop Recommendations

The recommendations suggest a way of proceeding in subsequent activities. Which TMMi process area is implemented first? Which part of a process area is to be addressed and in what way? The recommendations are formulated under the guidance of (internal or external) TMMi experts in the specific process area.

5.2.3 E – Establishing: The Establishing Phase

During this phase a detailed TMMi implementation plan is developed to implement the developed recommendations. The general goals as laid down in the Initiating phase are further specified in SMART goals. The recommendations are prioritized taking into account factors such as available resources, visibility, likely resistance, contribution to organizational goals, and so on. In the Establishing phase are the following activities:

- Set Priorities
- Develop Approach
- Plan Actions

Set Priorities

The first activity of this phase is to set priorities for the change effort. For example, it is futile to implement all five process areas of level 2 at once. When priorities are set, it is determined which process area(s) and which parts of them are implemented first. Several factors, such as available resources, visibility of the results, likely resistance, contribution to organizational goals, et cetera, should be taken into account.

Develop Approach

Using the recommendations and priorities, a strategy is developed for achieving the desired situation, the desired TMMi level, and the resources needed to achieve them are identified. Technical factors considered include new methods, techniques or resources. Attention must be paid to training, developing process descriptions and possible tool selection. In Appendix 2 an overview can be found of standards, methods and publications that can be used in a particular process area. Non-technical factors considered include knowledge and experience, implementation approach, resistance, support, sense of urgency, and the organization's culture, among other things.

Plan Actions

With the approach defined, detailed actions can be determined. Together with information taken from prior activities, these are combined into a plan including, among other things, actions, schedule, milestones, decision points, resources, responsibilities, measurement, tracking mechanisms, risks and implementation strategy.

5.2.4 A – Acting: The Acting Phase

This phase is about concrete activities, this is where the action is! The plan of approach must be executed. The recommendations must be specified in detail and must be implemented. Obviously this phase consumes most effort, because while developing the solution takes up about 30% of effort, implementing the solution takes up about 70% [Cannegieter]. In the Acting phase are the following activities:
- Create Solution
- Pilot/Test Solution
- Refine Solution
- Implement Solution.

Create Solution

The Acting phase begins with developing solutions to address the broadly outlined problems. These solutions should satisfy the purposes and practices of TMMi and contribute to achieving the desired situation. The solutions can include processes, templates, tools, knowledge, skills (training), information and support. The solutions, which can be quite complex, are often developed by improvement teams which include a TMMi expert. An approach using improvement teams that has proven to be successful is the improvement team relay [Zandhuis]. In an improvement team relay, a number of succeeding improvement teams develop and implement (parts of) the solution in a short time. Some advantages of the improvement team relay include reducing the lead time that would be required if only one overall improvement team was used, achieving results quickly and allowing for more exact guidance. Every improvement team needs to have a clear goal and be given a clear assignment by the management. As many employees as possible need to be involved in actually working out the solutions; an external consultant can provide guidance and content input.

Pilot/Test Solution
Following Tom Gilb's advice, "If you don't know what you are doing, don't do it on a large scale," the created solution first needs to be tested in one or more test projects. Sometimes only practical experience can show the exact effect of a solution. In pilots such as this, usually one or more test projects are appointed in which the improvements are implemented and evaluated before additional projects adopt the improvements.

Refine Solution
With the use of the results of the test or pilot, the solution can be optimized. Several iterations of the test-optimizing process may be necessary to reach a satisfactory solution that will work for all projects. A solution should be workable; waiting for a "perfect" solution may unnecessarily delay the implementation.

Implement Solution
Once the solutions are deemed workable, they can be implemented throughout the (test) organization. This is usually the most radical activity which can provoke much resistance. Several implementation approaches can be used, such as:

- big bang: all the organizational changes are implemented at the same time
- one project at a time: in every project the change is implemented at a set moment in time
- just in time: implementing the change when the process is executed.

No one implementation approach is better than another; the approach should be chosen based on the nature of the improvement and organizational circumstances. For a major change, implementation may require substantial time, resources, effort and attention from the management.

5.2.5 L – Learning: The Learning Phase

The Learning phase completes the improvement cycle. One of the goals of the IDEAL Model is to continuously improve the ability to implement change. In the Learning phase, the entire IDEAL experience is reviewed to determine what was accomplished, whether the intended goals were achieved and how the organization can implement change more effectively and efficiently. In the Learning phase are the following activities:

- Analyze and Validate
- Propose Future Actions.

Analyze and Validate

This activity answers several questions, such as:

- How did the improvement program go?
- What has been accomplished; have the initial goals been achieved?
- What worked well?
- What could be done more efficiently or effectively?

Using these questions for guidance, lessons learned are collected, analyzed, summarized and documented.

Propose Future Actions

Based upon the previous activity, recommendations are formulated which are intended to improve future improvement programs, whether or not based upon TMMi. These recommendations are provided to the higher management for consideration.

5.3 Critical Success Factors in a TMMi Implementation

5.3.1 Start of Improvement Process

The improvement process has already been discussed in general in the previous chapter. Several factors that are often found to be critical success factors in the initial phases are discussed below [Broekman/Van Veenendaal]. If these key factors are not met, this leads to an immediate and considerable risk for the improvement program that is to be executed. As indicated below, the key factors are all related to activities in the Initiating and Diagnosing phases of the IDEAL-model.

Test Policy

It is necessary to clearly define and record the goals of the improvement program. Why do we improve our test process? As indicated before, the goals of the change program are determined in the Initiating phase, and are subsequently developed or made concrete in the Establishing phase. The goals must be known to everyone involved. What is the direction the organization wants to take and why? All this should be recorded in the test policy, which is derived from the quality policy and the organizational policy. The test policy globally describes the organization's philosophy about testing. In TMMi the details of the test policy are elaborated upon within the process area Test Policy and Test Strategy.

Management Commitment

Is quality important enough to the organization? How does the organization deal with a system of inferior quality at a milestone? Is the organization driven by budget, deadline or quality? The answers to questions like these show the actual management commitment with regard to testing and quality. Without sufficient management commitment and an explicit sponsor at the management level an improvement process is highly likely to fail. Acquiring management commitment is discussed in the "Build Sponsorship" activity in the Initiating phase.

The Need to Improve

Before employees in an organization are willing to contribute to improvements, they must feel the need to improve. For example, this need can be to reduce the high number of defects when a system goes into production or to lower the time required to run a test project. The need to improve must clearly be communicated several times and preferably by the management. The goals need to support the defined need to improve.

Improvement is a Project

During the activity "Charter Infrastructure" (Initiating phase) the organization that will support the improvement process is set up. It is highly recommendable to choose a project structure with elements such as assignment, steering group, project lead, responsibilities, planning, milestones, deliverables, reports, et cetera. Change programs are often complex for several reasons. The authors' experience shows that creating an official project structure contributes to the change being taken seriously. As a defined project, the effort becomes visible in the organization and it's clear that the employees who contribute to the improvement program don't just do it as an "extra" but rather as an assigned project.

Availability of Resources

It is recommended to discuss the resources available for the change during the "Charter Infrastructure" activity instead of delaying it until the "Develop Approach" activity in the Establishing phase. It is important that the management realizes that choices must be made. For example, to allow employees four working hours a week to spend on improvement may sound good, but often proves not to work. When the employees working on the (test) project are pressed for time, they often do not have the extra four hours to do the improvement actions. An alternative can be to take a number of people off projects and assign them to the improvement program for minimally three days a week. This strategy leads to focus and progress and therefore to a timely delivery and measurable results.

Maturity of the (Development) Organization

In the "Characterize Current and Desired States" activity (Diagnosing phase) it is important to look at the test processes as well as the processes on which testing strongly depends. Without a minimum form of maturity in these processes, improving the test process will prove very difficult, although not impossible. One needs to look primarily at project planning, configuration management, requirements development and requirements management. Without a thorough project planning process, establishing a thorough test planning process will be very difficult, due to the many dependencies. When applying test design techniques, the quality of the requirements, the test basis, is of major importance. Any changes in the requirements must also be made known to the test team. Finally, the lack of configuration management often leads to non-reproducible findings or findings that "suddenly" reappear in a later release. These problems cannot be solved in the test process, but must be solved in the development process.

5.3.2 Establishing Improvements

The previous paragraph described how the important "first hurdle" must be overcome. To subsequently come to good results, momentum must be upheld in the program and everyone involved must stay focused. This paragraph describes a number of important factors that help to determine the success of a test improvement program.

Work on both Long Term and Short Term Goals

Process improvement is in essence a long term process. However, to retain motivation it is important to score so-called "quick wins" early in the process. The "supporters" within senior management also want to show a periodic success to justify their support for the improvement team. Whenever success is achieved, for example during the pilot, this must be communicated clearly and repeatedly. By formulating success using examples that are specific to the organization or its individual employees, the enthusiasm for the improvement program generally grows.

Deal with Resistance, use Marketing

Initially, most people naturally resist change. Trying to push through that resistance often has the opposite effect. It is better to try to convince them by marketing the improvement program. For example, publish the achieved results or stories from people who have experienced the positive effects of the improvements in a regular newsletter. Whenever resistance is detected, it is advisable to talk about it with the employee concerned. In this conversation it is important that the change manager also listens to the objections of the employee. Resistance is often a result of uncertainty about the need and objectives of the change project, unfamiliarity with the approach of the change project or uncertainty about the employee's own situation.

Use What is Available in the Organization

Even though apparently there is much that needs improving, this does not mean everything is wrong as it is. Many unsuccessful attempts to improve have been started; sometimes some test projects are executed in a more controlled way than others are. It is likely that several employees have had good ideas, but they have not succeeded in deploying them. Use those people and ideas. Resistance is less when changes are derived from one's own ranks.

Dedicate Time and Resources

The test process improvement project must be seen as a fulltime job and not as "something on the side". When results need to be achieved in a project, it is fatal when people can work on it for only a short time and then must leave because another, more important project demands their attention.

Define the Role of External Consultants

External consultants can positively add to the project with their knowledge and experience. When they have been deployed, "dedicated" to the improvement project, they can keep it going despite other organization schedules. However, the external consultants must not decide on the working procedures; this must be decided by the employees of the organization itself. This is why in every improvement program internal employees should be the primary resources involved, supported as needed by external consultants. In addition, improvements must be anchored in the organization so the effort and momentum continues after the consultant leaves.

Guard Consistency

Guard the consistency between the several improved parts. The total sum of all improvements must integrate and work as one.

5.4 Test Process Improvement Manifesto

In addition to the improvement process as described in the IDEAL framework and the critical success factors that one needs to take into account during the implementation process, the Test Process Improvement Manifesto [Van Veenendaal] also provides a number of interesting recommendations. The Test Process Improvement Manifesto identifies a number of principles that can make a difference in a test process improvement project. These principles / recommendations have been defined based on an analysis of successful test improvement projects in various domains.

Test Process Improvement Manifesto
- Flexibility *over Detailed Processes*
- Best practices *over Templates*
- Deployment orientation *over Process orientation*
- Peer reviews *over Quality Assurance (departments)*
- Business-driven *over Model-driven*

Flexibility over Detailed Processes

In general, having defined processes supports an organization. Only something that is defined can be improved. It guides new engineers and acts as corporate memory. However, building processes that are too rigorous takes away the "people values". Good testers have the skills to act based on the context of a problem and perceive testing to be a challenging job. Supporting processes are needed but the employed processes should give enough flexibility and freedom to testers to allow them to think for themselves and find the best way forward. The ideal is "just enough process".

Best Practices over Templates

Templates are great but it is even better to provide examples of how they should be used. What provides more support; a test plan template or three test plan best practices? Experienced testers will choose the latter. When doing test process improvement it's important to focus on getting a best practices library set up as soon as possible instead of overspending on defining templates. The best practices may not be the best in the industry, but they may be the best for your organization. If something better comes along, they can be replaced. This is what supports testing and makes process improvement work.

Deployment Orientation over Process Orientation

Building process is easy; it's been done many times and there are numerous examples to be found. However, getting the processes deployed and thereby changing someone's behavior is the hard part. Process improvement is all about change management. Test improvement plans sometimes erroneously focus almost entirely on defining the testing processes. In successful improvement projects at least 70% of the improvement effort is spent on deployment – "getting the job done". Defining the processes is the easy part and should only account for a small percentage of the effort and focus.

Peer Reviews over Quality Assurance (Departments)

Communicating and providing feedback are essential to project success. It is exactly this which peer reviews, if applied well, do. In principle, quality assurance officers also evaluate documents and provide feedback to engineers but they tend to focus on conformance to templates and defined processes, partly because they are somewhat distanced from the testing profession. This reduces the value they contribute. Peer reviews, when done by qualified peers, provide pertinent feedback and advice for the given application which is generally more beneficial than just adherence to a template.

Business-Driven Over Model-Driven

Just trying to get to TMMi level 2 or 3 without understanding the business context will always fail in the short or long term. The improvement team must understand the business problem in order to determine how to address the improvements. Whatever you do, make sure you know why you are doing it. What is the business problem you are trying to address? What is the test policy supported by management? When addressing a certain practice from an improvement model, there are most often many different ways to comply. The business problem (poor product quality, long test execution lead time, costs, etc.) will determine which one to choose. Process improvement must be constantly reviewed against the business drivers and test policy to ensure compliance.

Appendix A

Relationship Between TMMi and CMMI

CMMI Process Areas that Support a TMMi Implementation

Although TMMi can be used and implemented in isolation, it is also positioned as a complementary model. As a result, in many cases CMMI process areas can support a TMMi implementation. An overview of the CMMI process areas (in italics) that are specifically relevant is provided hereafter. Their relationship to the TMMi process areas is summarized in table A.1.

Table A.1 Support from CMMI process areas for TMMI process areas

		CMMI L2						CMMI L3						CMMI L4		CMMI L5	
		CM	MA	PMC	PP	PPQA	REQM	OPD	OPF	OT	RD	RSKM	VER	OPP	QPM	CAR	OID
TMMI L2	2.1 Test Policy and Strategy		x														
	2.2. Test Planning				x		x					x					
	2.3 Test Monitoring and Control			x								x					
	2.4 Test Design and Execution						x										
	2.5 Test Environment										x						
TMMI L3	3.1 Test Organization								x								
	3.2 Test Training Program									x							
	3.3 Test Lifecycle and Integration				x		x	x				x					
	3.4 Non-Functional Testing						x										
	3.5 Peer Reviews												x				

Table A.1 Support from CMMI process areas for TMMI process areas		CMMI L2						CMMI L3						CMMI L4		CMMI L5	
		CM	MA	PMC	PP	PPQA	REQM	OPD	OPF	OT	RD	RSKM	VER	OPP	QPM	CAR	OID
TMMI L4	4.1 Test Measurement		x														
	4.2 Product Quality Evaluation														x		
	4.3 Advanced Peer Reviews																
TMMI L5	5.1 Defect Prevention															x	
	5.2 Quality Control													x			
	5.3 Test Process Optimization																x
GG's	Generic Goal 2	x			x	x											
	Generic Goal 3		x					x	x								

CMMI Level 2 process areas

Configuration Management (CM)

The purpose of Configuration Management is to establish and maintain the integrity of work products using configuration identification, configuration control, configuration status accounting, and configuration audits. The CMMI Configuration Management process can implement TMMi generic practice GP2.6 Manage Configuration in full for all project-related process areas as well as some of the organizational process areas.

Measurement and Analysis (MA)

The purpose of Measurement and Analysis is to develop and sustain a measurement capability that is used to support management information needs. The CMMI Measurement and Analysis process area provides support for the implementation of the SG 3 Establish Test Performance indicators of the TMMi process area Test Policy and Strategy. This CMMI process area also provides support for the implementation of the TMMi process area Test Measurement. The measurement infrastructure and practices can be re-used for test measurement. It may be practical to implement the test measurement program as a supplement to the general measurement program. Finally, for all processes the CMMI Measurement and Analysis provides general guidance about measuring, analyzing, and recording information that can be used in establishing measures for monitoring actual performance of the processes thereby supporting the implementation of TMMi generic practice GP 3.2 Collect Improvement Information.

Project Monitoring and Control (PMC)

The purpose of Project Monitoring and Control is to provide an understanding of the project's progress so that appropriate corrective actions can be taken when the project's performance deviates significantly from the plan. This process area provides support for the implementation of the TMMi process area Test Monitoring and Control. Project management practices can be re-used for test management.

Project Planning (PP)

The purpose of Project Planning is to establish and maintain plans that define project activities. The CMMI Project Planning process area provides support for the implementation of the TMMi process areas Test Planning and Test Lifecycle and Integration (SG3 Establish a Master Test Plan). Project management practices can be re-used for test management.

Process and Product Quality Assurance (PPQA)

The purpose of Process and Product Quality Assurance (PPQA) is to provide staff and management with objective insight into processes and associated work products. The CMMI PPQA process can implement the generic practice GP2.9 Objectively Evaluate Adherence in full for all process areas.

Requirements Management (REQM)

The purpose of Requirements Management is to manage the requirements of the project's products and product components and to identify inconsistencies between those requirements and the project's plans and work products. The implementation of the Requirement Management process area is a constraint for managing derived (work) products, such as the product risk analysis and test designs, and keeping them up-to-date and consistent. The practices regarding maintaining traceability possibly can be re-used within the Test Design and Execution TMMi process area.

CMMI Level 3 process areas

Organizational Process Definition (OPD)

The purpose of Organizational Process Definition is to establish and maintain a usable set of organizational process assets and work environment standards. This CMMI process area provides support for the implementation of the TMMi process area Test Lifecycle and Integration, especially for SG1 Establish Organizational Test Process Assets. The CMMI process area Organizational Process Definition can also support the implementation of generic practice GP3.1 Establish a Defined Process by establishing the organizational process assets needed to implement GP3.1.

Organizational Process Focus (OPF)

The purpose of Organizational Process Focus is to plan, implement, and deploy organizational process improvements based on a thorough understanding of the current strengths and weaknesses of the organization's processes and process assets. This CMMI process area provides support for the implementation of the TMMi process area Test Organization, especially for SG4 Determine, Plan and Implement Test Process Improvements and SG5 Deploy Organizational Test Processes and Incorporate Lessons Learned. It also provides support for the implementation of the TMMi generic practices GP3.2 Collect Improvement Information since it establishes an organizational measurement repository.

Organizational Training (OT)

The purpose of Organizational Training is to develop the skills and knowledge of people so they can perform their roles effectively and efficiently. This CMMI process area provides support for the implementation of the TMMi process area Test Training Program.

Requirements Development (REQD)

The purpose of Requirements Development is to produce and analyze customer, product, and product component requirements. Practices from this CMMI process area can be re-used when developing test environment requirements within the process area Test Environment.

Risk Management (RSKM)

The purpose of Risk Management is to identify potential problems before they occur so that risk-handling activities can be planned and invoked as needed across the life of the product or project to mitigate adverse impacts on achieving objectives. Practices from this CMMI process area can be re-used for identifying and controlling product risk and test project risks within the process areas Test Planning and Test Monitoring and Control.

Verification (VER)

The purpose of Verification is to ensure that selected work products meet their specified requirements. The practices within SG2 Perform Peer Reviews of this CMMI process area provide support for the implementation of the TMMi process area Peer Reviews.

CMMI Level 4 process areas

Organizational Process Performance (OPP)

The purpose of Organizational Process Performance is to establish and maintain a quantitative understanding of the performance of the organization's set of standard processes in support of quality and process-performance objectives, and to provide the process performance data baselines, and models to quantitatively manage the organization's projects. This CMMI process area provides support for the implementation of the TMMi process area Quality Control, especially SG1 Establish a Statistically Controlled Test Process.

Quantitative Project Management (QPM)

The purpose of Quantitative Project Management is to quantitatively manage the project's defined process to achieve the project's established quality and process-performance objectives. This CMMI process area provides support for the implementation of the TMMi process area Product Quality Evaluation, both for SG1 Measurable Project Goals for Product Quality and their Priorities are Established, and SG2 Actual Progress Toward Achieving Product Quality Goals is Quantified and Managed.

CMMI Level 5 process areas

Causal Analysis and Resolution (CAR)

The purpose of Causal Analysis and Resolution is to identify causes of defects and other problems and take action to prevent them from occurring in the future. This CMMI process area provides support for the implementation of the TMMi process area Defect Prevention.

Organizational Innovation and Deployment (OID)

The purpose of Organizational Innovation and Deployment is to select and deploy incremental and innovative improvements that measurably improve the organization´s processes and technologies. This CMMI process area provides support for the implementation of the TMMi process area Test Process Optimization.

TMMi Process Areas that Support Other Parts of TMMi

In addition to using parts of CMMI, TMMi process areas can also be used to support the implementation of the TMMi generic practices. An overview of the TMMi process areas in alphabetical order (in italics) that are specifically relevant is provided below.

Test Lifecycle and Integration

This TMMi process area can provide support for the implementation of the generic practice GP3.2 Collect Improvement Information, since it establishes an organizational test process database. Test lifecycle and Integration also supports the implementation of generic practice GP3.1 Establish a Defined Process, by establishing the organizational process assets needed to implement GP3.1.

Test Measurement
For all processes, the Test Measurement process area can provide general guidance about measuring, analyzing, and recording information that can be used in establishing measures for monitoring actual performance of the processes thereby supporting the implementation of TMMi generic practice GP 3.2 Collect Improvement Information.

Test Monitoring and Control
The Test Monitoring and Control process area can implement the generic practice GP2.8 Monitor and Control the Process, in full for all process areas.

Test Planning
The Test Planning process can implement GP2.2 Plan the Process, in full for all project-related process areas. It may also support the generic practice G2.7 Identify and Involve the Relevant Stakeholders, for all project related process areas by planning the involvement of identified stakeholders and documenting those in the test plan.

Test Training Program
The Test Training Program process supports the implementation of TMMi generic practice GP2.5 Train People, for all process areas by making the organization-wide training program available to those who will perform or support the processes.

TMMi Process Areas that Support a CMMI Implementation
CMMI contains two process areas that focus on testing: Verification and Validation. The purpose of Verification is to ensure that selected work products meet their specified requirements. The purpose of Validation is to demonstrate that a product or product component fulfills its intended use when placed in its intended environment. The goals of the CMMI process areas Verification and Validation are fulfilled by implementing the TMMi level 2 process areas and the process area Peer Review at TMMi level 3. Note that one important comment needs to be made. The CMMI process areas Verification and Validation have a very different test objective. The implementation of the TMMi level 2 process areas and Peer Reviews from TMMi level 3 only fulfill the requirements of Verification and Validation when the test policy, test strategy and test approach cover the test objectives from both Verification and Validation.

Appendix B

Sources to Support TMMi Implementation

Simply speaking, TMMi defines the requirements for mature testing processes, grouped by process area. TMMi therefore "only" describes the characteristics of mature testing processes, not the concrete detailed implementation of those processes. Various standards, methods and techniques have been published that an organization can use to implement their processes such that they meet the TMMi requirements. Per process area the authors identify which standards, methods or techniques are highly useful during the implementation of that process area and where they are published.

TMMi Level 2 Process Areas

PA 2.1 Test Policy and Strategy

Specific Goal	Supporting literature
SG 1 Establish a Test Policy	[Black09] – par. 3.3 [ISTQB Advanced Syllabus] – par. 3.2 [TestGrip]
SG 2 Establish a Test Strategy	[Black] – par. 3.3 [Foundations of SW Testing] – par. 5.2 [ISTQB Advanced Syllabus] – par. 3.2
SG 3 Establish Test Performance Indicators	[ISTQB Advanced Syllabus] – par. 3.7 [ISTQB Expert Syllabus] – par. 4.4 [Goal/Question/Metric]

PA 2.2 Test Planning

Specific Goal	Supporting literature
SG 1 Perform a Product Risk Assessment	[Black04] – Chapter 2 [ISTQB Advanced Syllabus] – par. 3.9 [PRISMA] [RRBT] – Chapter 5
SG 2 Establish a Test Approach	[Foundations of SW Testing] – par. 4.6 [PRISMA] – par. 7.6 [TMap] – par. 15.3.5

SG 3 Establish Test Estimates	[Black04] – Chapters 3 and 5 [ISTQB Advanced Syllabus] – par. 3.4 [RRBT] – Chapter 6 [Testing Practitioner] – Chapter 7
SG 4 Develop a Test Plan	[IEEE 829] – Chapter 9 [RRBT] – Appendix E [TMapNext] – Chapter 6
SG 5 Obtain Commitment to the Test Plan	No specific supporting literature

PA 2.3 Test Monitoring and Control

Specific Goal	Supporting literature
SG 1 Monitor Test Progress Against Plan	[Black04] – Chapter 13 [IEEE 829] – Chapters 15 and 16 [ISTQB Advanced Syllabus] – par. 3.6 [RRBT] – Chapters 10 and 12
SG 2 Monitor Product Quality Against Plan and Expectations	[IEEE 829] – Chapters 15 and 16 [ISTQB Advanced Syllabus] – par. 3.6 [RRBT] – Chapters 10 and 12 [Testing Practitioner] – Chapter 6
SG 3 Manage Corrective Action to Closure	[ISTQB Advanced Syllabus] – par. 3.6

PA 2.4 Test Design and Execution

Specific Goal	Supporting literature
SG 1 Perform Test Analysis and Design Using Test Design Techniques	[Bath/McKay] – par. 3.2.2 and Chapters 4, 5, 6 and 7 [BS7925/2] [Copeland] – Section I and II [Foundations of SW Testing] – par. 1.4 and Chapter 4 [IEEE 829] – Chapters 10 and 11 [ISTQB Advanced Syllabus] – par. 2.4 and Chapter 4 [Testing Practitioner] – Chapters 13 and 14
SG 2 Perform Test Implementation	[Bath/McKay] – par. 3.2.3 [Foundations of SW Testing] – par. 1.4 [IEEE 829] – Chapter 12 [ISTQB Advanced Syllabus] – par. 2.5

SG 3 Perform Test Execution	[Bath/McKay] – par. 3.2.3 [Black04] – Chapter 13 and 14 [Foundations of SW Testing] – par. 1.4 [IEEE 829] – Chapters 13 and 14 [IEEE 1044] [ISTQB Advanced Syllabus] – par. 2.5 [Testing Practitioner] – Chapter 17
SG 4 Manage Test Incidents to Closure	[Bath/McKay] – Chapter 19 [Foundations of SW Testing] – par. 5.6 [IEEE 1044] [ISTQB Advanced Syllabus] – Chapter 7 [RRBT] – Chapter 11 [Testing Practitioner] – Chapter 17

PA 2.5 Test Environment

Specific Goal	Supporting literature
SG 1 Develop Test Environment Requirements	[Black04] – Chapter 10 [IREB] [Robertson/Robertson] [TMapNext] – par. 8.4
SG 2 Perform Test Environment Implementation	[Black04] – Chapter 10 [Foundations of SW Testing] – par. 1.4 [TestFrame] – Chapter 8 [TMapNext] – par. 8.4 [ISTQB Advanced Syllabus] – par. 2.5
SG 3 Manage and Control Test Environments	[TestFrame] – Chapter 8 [TMapNext] – par. 8.4 [TMap] – Chapter 22

TMMi Level 3 Process Areas

PA 3.1 Test Organization

Specific Goal	Supporting literature
SG 1 Establish a Test Organization	[Foundations of SW Testing] – par. 5.1 [RRBT] – Chapter 8 [TMapNext] – par. 8.3
SG 2 Establish Test Functions for Test Specialists	[Foundations of SW Testing] – par. 5.1 [RRBT] – Chapter 8 [TMap] – Chapter 19

SG 3 Establish Test Career Paths	[Black04] – Chapter 9 [Testing Practitioner] – Chapter 24
SG 4 Determine, Plan and Implement Test Process Improvements	[IDEAL] [ISTQB Expert Syllabus] – Chapter 6
SG 5 Deploy the Organizational Test Process and Incorporate Lessons Learned	[Black04] – Chapter 17 [Foundations of SW Testing] – par. 1.4 [IDEAL] [ISTQB Expert Syllabus] – Chapters 6 and 8 [RRBT] – Chapter 13

PA 3.2 Test Training Program

Specific Goal	Supporting literature
SG 1 Establish an Organizational Test Training Capability	[ISTQB Advanced Syllabus] – par. 10.2 [TMap] – par. 20.2
SG 2 Provide Necessary Test Training	No specific supporting literature

PA 3.3 Test Lifecycle and Integration

Specific Goal	Supporting literature
SG 1 Establish Organizational Test Process Assets	[CMMI DEV] – process areas Organizational Process Focus and Organizational Process Definition
SG 2 Integrate the Test Lifecycle Models with the Development Models	[Foundations of SW Testing] – Chapter 2 [ISTQB Advanced Syllabus] – par. 1.2
SG 3 Establish a Master Test Plan	[IEEE 829] – Chapter 8 [ISTQB Advanced Syllabus] – par. 3.2 [TMapNext] – Chapter 5

PA 3.4 Non-Functional Testing

Specific Goal	Supporting literature
SG 1 Perform a Non-Functional Product Risk Assessment	[Black04] – Chapter 2 [ISO 9126-1] [ISTQB Advanced Syllabus] – par. 3.9 [RRBT] – Chapter 5
SG 2 Establish a Non-Functional Test Approach	[ISTQB Advanced Syllabus] – Chapter 5 [TMap] – Chapter 12

SG 3 Perform Non-Functional Test Analysis and Design	[Bath/McKay] – par. 3.2.2 and Chapters 11, 12, 13, 14, 15 and 16. [Foundations of SW Testing] – par. 1.4 [IEEE 829] – Chapters 10 and 11 [ISTQB Advanced Syllabus] – par. 2.4 and Chapter 5 [Testing Practitioner] – Chapters 15 and 16 [Testingstandards] – Non-Functional Testing
SG 4 Perform Non-Functional Test Implementation	[Bath/McKay] – par. 3.2.3 [Foundations of SW Testing] – par. 1.4 [IEEE 829] – Chapter 12 [ISTQB Advanced Syllabus] – par. 2.5
SG 5 Perform Non-Functional Test Execution	[Bath/McKay] – par. 3.2.3 [Foundations of SW Testing] – par. 1.4 [IEEE 829] – Chapters 13 and 14 [IEEE 1044] [ISTQB Advanced Syllabus] – par. 2.5 [Testing Practitioner] – Chapter 17

PA 3.5 Peer reviews

Specific Goal	Supporting literature
SG 1 Establish a Peer Review Approach	[Foundations of SW Testing] – par. 3.2 [Gilb and Graham] [Testing Practitioner] – Chapters 8, 9 and 10 [IEEE 1028]
SG 2 Perform Peer Reviews	[Foundations of SW Testing] – par. 3.2 [Gilb and Graham] [Testing Practitioner] – Chapters 8, 9 and 10 [IEEE 1028]

TMMi Level 4 Process Areas

PA 4.1 Test Measurement

Specific Goal	Supporting literature
SG 1 Align Test Measurement and Analysis Activities	[AMI] – Chapters 3 and 4 [Burnstein] – Chapter 11 [Goal/Question/Metric] – Chapters 5 and 6 [TMapNext] – Chapter 13

SG 2 Provide Test Measurement Results	[AMI] – Chapters 5 and 6
	[Burnstein] - Chapter 11
	[Goal/Question/Metric] – Chapters 7 and 8
	[TMapNext] – Chapter 13

PA 4.2 Product Quality Evaluation

Specific Goal	Supporting literature
SG 1 Measurable Project Goals for Product Quality and their Priorities are Established	[Burnstein] – par. 11.3
	[Bath/McKay] - Chapters 11, 12, 13, 14, 15 and 16
	[ISO 9126-2]
	[ISO 9126-3]
	[RRBT] – annex B
	[Testingstandards] – Non-Functional Testing
	[Trienekens/Van Veenendaal] – Chapter 2 and annex B
SG 2 Actual Progress Toward Achieving the Project's Product Quality Goals is Quantified and Managed	[AMI] – Chapters 5 and 6
	[Burnstein] – par. 11.3
	[Goal/Question/Metric] – Chapters 7 and 8

PA 4.3 Advanced Reviews

Specific Goal	Supporting literature
SG 1 Coordinate the Peer Review Approach with the Dynamic Test Approach	[PRISMA] – par. 7.6
SG 2 Measure Product Quality Early in the Lifecycle by Means of Peer Reviews	[Gilb05]
	[Gilb08]
	[Testing Practitioner] – Chapter 9
SG 3 Adjust the Test Approach Based on Review Results Early in the Lifecycle	[AMI] – Chapters 5 and 6
	[Goal/Question/Metric] – Chapters 7 and 8
	[ISTQB Advanced Syllabus] – par. 3.9.3

TMMi Level 5 Process Areas

PA 5.1 Defect Prevention

Specific Goal	Supporting literature
SG 1 Determine Common Causes of Defects	[Burnstein] – Chapter 13 [Gilb and Graham] – Chapter 7 [Humprey] – Chapter 17 [IEEE 1044] [ISTQB Expert Syllabus] – par. 4.2
SG 2 Prioritize and Define Actions to Systematically Eliminate Root Causes of Defects	[Burnstein] – Chapter 13 [Gilb and Graham] – Chapter 7 [Humprey] – Chapter 17 [ISTQB Expert Syllabus] – par. 4.2

PA 5.2 Quality Control

Specific Goal	Supporting literature
SG 1 Establish a Statistically Controlled Test Process	[Burnstein] – par. 15.2 – 15.4 [Oakland] – Chapter 9 [Weller]
SG 2 Testing is Performed using Statistical Methods	[Burnstein] – par. 12.2 – 12.7 [Musa/Ackerman] [Musa87] [Musa93] [Walton]

PA 5.3 Test Process Optimization

Specific Goal	Supporting literature
SG 1 Select Test Process Improvements	[Burnstein] par. 15.5 [IDEAL] [ISTQB Expert Syllabus] – Chapter 6
SG 2 New Technologies are Evaluated to Determine their Impact on the Testing Process	[Burnstein] – 15.6 [Daich] [IDEAL]
SG 3 Deploy Test Improvements	[IDEAL] [ISTQB Expert Syllabus] – Chapters 6 and 8
SG 4 Establish Re-use of High Quality Test Assets	[Burnstein] 15.7 [Hollenbach/Frakes]

References

The list below contains both the literature referenced in the text and the literature references (recommendations) from Appendix B.

- [AMI] K. Pulford, A. Kuntzmann, S. Shirlaw (1995), *A quantitative approach to Software Management – The AMI handbook*, Addison-Wesley
- [Bath/McKay] G. Bath and J. McKay (2008), *The Software Test Engineer's Handbook*, Rockynook
- [Beizer] B. Beizer (1990), *Software Testing Techniques, 2nd edition*, Van Nostrand Reinhold
- [Black04] R. Black (2004), *Critical Testing Processes – Plan Prepare, Perform, Perfect*, Addison-Wesley
- [Black09] R. Black (2009) *Advanced Software Testing, Vol. 2, Guide to the ISTQB Advanced Certification as an Advanced Test Manager*, Rockynook
- [Broekman/van Veenendaal] B. Broekman and E. van Veenendaal (2007), Test process improvement (in Dutch), in: *Software testen in Nederland; 10 jaar TESTNET*, H. van Loenhoud (red.), Academic Service
- [BS7925/2] BS 7925/2 (1997), *Standard for Software Component Testing*, British Computer Society Specialist Interest Group in Software Testing
- [Burnstein] I. Burnstein (2002), *Practical Software Testing; A process-oriented approach*, Springer
- [Cannegieter] J.J. Cannegieter (2003), *Software Process Improvement (in Dutch)*, SDU Publishing
- [CMMI DEV] SEI (2008), *CMMI for Development Version 1.2*, CMU/SEI-2006-TR-008, Software Engineering Institute
- [Copeland] L. Copeland (2003), *A Practitioner's Guide to Software Test Design*, Artech House Publishers
- [Daich] G. Daich, G. Price, B. Ragland and M. Dawood (1994), *Software Test Technologies Report*, August 1994, Software Technology Support Center (STSC)
- [Foundations of SW Testing] D. Graham, E. van Veenendaal, I. Evans, R. Black (2008), Foundations of Software Testing (2nd edition), Cengage Learning,
- [Gelperin/Hetzel] D. Gelperin en W.C. Hetzel (1988), The growth in Software Testing, in: *Communications of the ACM*, 1988
- [Goal/Question/Metric] R. van Solingen and E. Berghout (1999), *The Goal/Question/Metric method*, McGrawHill
- [Gilb05] T. Gilb (2005), *Agile Specification Quality Control: Shifting emphasis from cleanup to sampling defects*, Incose
- [Gilb08] T. Gilb (2008), Rule-based Design Reviews, in: *Testing Experience*, June 2008
- [Gilb/Graham] T. Gilb and D. Graham (1993), Software Inspection, Addison-Wesley
- [Hollenbach/Frakes] C. Hollenbach and W. Frakes (1996), Software process re-use in an industrial setting, in: *Proceedings Fourth International Conference on Software Reuse*, Orlando, Florida, April 1996s
- [Humprey] W.s. Humprey (1989), *Managing the Software Process*, Addison-Wesley
- [IDEAL] SEI (1997), *IDEAL: A Users Guide for Software Process Improvement*, Software Engineering Institute
- [IEEE 610] IEEE Std 610 (1990), *Standard Glossary of Software Engineering Terminology*, IEEE Computer Society
- [IEEE 829] IEEE Std 829 (2008) *Standard For Software and System Test Documentation*, IEEE Computer Society
- [IEEE 1008] IEEE Std 1008 (1987), *Standard for Software Unit Testing*, IEEE Computer Society

- [IEEE 1028] IEEE Std 1028 (1997), *Standard for Software Review*, IEEE Computer Society
- [IEEE 1044] IEEE Std 1044 (1993), Standard Classification for Software Anomalies, *IEEE Computer Society*
- [IREB] IREB (2009), *IREB Certified Professional for Requirements Engineering Foundation Syllabus,* International Requirements Engineering Board
- [ISO 9000] ISO 9000 (2005), *Quality Management Systems – Fundamentals and Vocabulary,* International Organization of Standardization
- [ISO 9126-1] ISO/IEC 9126-1 (2001), *Software engineering – Software Product Quality – Part 1: Quality Characteristics and sub-characteristics,* International Organization of Standardization
- [ISO 9126-2] ISO/IEC 9126-1 (2001), *Software engineering – Software Product Quality – Part 2: External metrics,* International Organization of Standardization
- [ISO 9126-3] ISO/IEC 9126-1 (2000), *Software engineering – Software Product Quality – Part 3: Internal metrics,* International Organization of Standardization
- [ISTQB Advanced Syllabus] ISTQB (2007), *Certified Tester, Advanced Level Syllabus,* International Software Testing Qualifications Board
- [ISTQB Expert Syllabus] ISTQB (2009), *Certified Tester, Expert Level Syllabus; Improving the Testing Process – Implementing Improvement and Change,* International Software Testing Qualifications Board
- [ISTQB Foundation Syllabus] ISTQB (2010), *Certified Tester Foundation Level Syllabus,* International Software Testing Qualifications Board
- [ISTQB Glossary] E. van Veenendaal (ed.) (2010), *Standard Glossary of Terms Used in Software Testing Version 2.1,* International Software Testing Qualifications Board
- [ITAM] Improve Quality Services (2009), *Improve TMMi Assessment Method Version 1.2,* internal document Improve Quality Services BV
- [Musa/Ackerman] J. Musa and A. Ackermann (1989), Quantifying software verification: when to stop testing, in: *IEEE Software*, Vol. 6, No. 3, May 1989
- [Musa87] J. Musa, A. Ackermann and K. Olomoto (1987), *Software Reliability: Measurement, Prediction, and Application,* McGraw-Hill
- [Musa93] J. Musa (1993), Operational Profiles in software reliability engineering, in: *IEEE Software,* Vol. 10, No. 3, 1993
- [Oakland] J.S. Oakland (1995), *Total Quality Management – The route to improving performance,* Butterworth Heinemann
- [Paulk] M.C. Paulk, C.V. Weber, B. Curtis, M.B. Chrissis (1994), *The Capability Maturity Model,* Addison-Wesley
- [PRISMA] E. van Veenendaal (2009), *Practical Risk-Based Testing – Product RISk MAnangement: the PRISMA method,* white-paper Improve Quality Services BV, May 2009
- [Robertson/Robertson] S. Robertson and J. Robertson (2006), *Mastering the Requirements Process 2nd edition,* Addison-Wesley
- [RRBT] I. Prinkster, B. van der Burgt, D. Janssen, E. van Veenendaal (2006), *Successful Test Management; An Integral Approach,* Springer
- [Sogeti] Sogeti (2009), *TPI Next – Business Driven Test Process Improvement,* UTN Publishers
- [TestFrame] C. Schotanus (2008), *TestFrame, An Approach to Structured Testing,* Springer
- [TestGrip] R. Marselis, J. van Rooyen, C. Schotanus (2007), *TestGrip - Gaining control on IT quality and processes through test policy and test organization,* Logica
- [Testingstandards] www.testingstandards.co.uk - Non-Functional Testing
- [Testing Practitioner] E. van Veenendaal (2002), *The Testing Practitioner,* UTN Publishers

- [TMap] M. Pol, R. Teunissen, E. van Veenendaal (2002), *Software Testing, A guide to the TMap Approach,* Addison-Wesley
- [TMapNext] T. Koomen, L. van der Aalst, B. Broekman, M. Vroon (2006), *TMapNext for result driven testing,* UTN Publishers
- [Trienekens/Van Veenendaal] J. Trienekens and E. van Veenendaal (1997), *Software Quality from a Business Perspective – directions and advanced approaches,* Kluwer Bedrijfsinformatie
- [Van Solingen] R. van Solingen (2004), Measuring the ROI of Software Process Improvement, in: *IEEE Software,* May/June 2004
- [Van Veenendaal] E. van Veenendaal (2008), Test Process Improvement Manifesto, in: *Testing Experience,* Issue 04, 2008
- [Van Veenendaal/Cannegieter] E. van Veenendaal and J.J. Cannegieter (2010), *The Little TMMi (in Dutch),* SDU Publishing
- [Walton] G. Walton, J. Poore and C. Trammell, Statistical testing of software based on a usage model, in: *Software Practice and Experience,* Vol. 25, No. 1, 1995
- [Weller] E. Weller (2000), Practical Applications of statistical process control, in: *IEEE Software,* Vol. 14, No. 3, 2000
- [Zandhuis] J. Zandhuis (2009), *Improvement team relay, agile improvements (in Dutch),* SPIder Conference October, 6th 2009

Glossary

Black-box testing	Testing, either functional or non-functional, without reference to the internal structure of the component or system.
Configuration management	A discipline applying technical and administrative direction and surveillance to: identify and document the functional and physical characteristics of a configuration item, control changes to those characteristics, record and report change processing and implementation status, and verify compliance with specified requirements. [IEEE 610]
Continuous representation	A capability maturity model structure wherein capability levels provide a recommended order for approaching process improvement within specified process areas. [CMMI DEV]
Defect	A flaw in a component or system that can cause the component or system to fail to perform its required function, e.g., an incorrect statement or data definition. A defect, if encountered during execution, may cause a failure of the component or system.
Dynamic testing	Testing that involves the execution of the software of a component or system.
Entry criteria	The set of generic and specific conditions for permitting a process to go forward with a defined task, e.g., test phase. The purpose of entry criteria is to prevent a task from starting which would entail more (wasted) effort compared to the effort needed to remove the failed entry criteria. [Gilb and Graham]
Exit criteria	The set of generic and specific conditions, agreed upon with the stakeholders, for permitting a process to be officially completed. The purpose of exit criteria is to prevent a task from being considered completed when there are still outstanding parts of the task which have not been finished. Exit criteria are used to report against and to plan when to stop testing. [After Gilb and Graham]
Feature	An attribute of a component or system specified or implied by requirements documentation (for exam-

97

ple reliability, usability or design constraints). [After IEEE 1008]

Formal assessment   A TMMi assessment that results in a detailed understanding regarding the extent to which an organization complies with the TMMi goals at a certain TMMi level, and therefore is able to issue a formal and completely verifiable statement regarding compliance to a certain TMMi maturity level.

Generic goal   A required model component that describes the characteristics that must be present to institutionalize the processes that implement a process area. [CMMI DEV]

Generic practice   An expected model component that is considered important in achieving the associated generic goal. The generic practices associated with a generic goal describe the activities that are expected to result in achievement of the generic goal and contribute to the institutionalization of the processes associated with a process area. [CMMI DEV]

Higher level management   The person or persons who provide the policy and overall guidance for the process, but do not to provide direct day-to-day monitoring and controlling of the process. Such persons belong to a level of management in the organization above the intermediate level responsible for the process and can be (but are not necessarily) senior managers. [CMMI DEV]

Horizontal traceability   The tracing of requirements for a test level through the layers of test documentation (e.g., test plan, test design specification, test case specification and test procedure specification or test script).

IDEAL   An organizational improvement model that serves as a roadmap for initiating, planning, and implementing improvement actions. The IDEAL model is named for the five phases it describes: initiating, diagnosing, establishing, acting, and learning.

Informal assessment   A TMMi assessment that results in a high level understanding regarding the extent to which an organization complies with the TMMi goals at a certain TMMi level, and therefore is able to define improvement areas and/or evaluate the progress of a TMMi improvement process.

Incident	Any event occurring that requires investigation. [After IEEE 1008]
Institutionalization	The ingrained way of doing business that an organization follows routinely as part of its corporate culture.
Intake test	A special instance of a smoke test to decide if the component or system is ready for detailed and further testing. An intake test is typically carried out at the start of the test execution phase.
Master test plan	A test plan that typically addresses multiple test levels.
Maturity level	Degree of process improvement across a predefined set of process areas in which all goals in the set are attained. [CMMI DEV]
Measure	The number or category assigned to an attribute of an entity by making a measurement. [ISO 14598]
Measurement	The process of assigning a number or category to an entity to describe an attribute of that entity. [ISO 14598]
Peer review	A review of a software work product by colleagues of the producer of the product for the purpose of identifying defects and improvements. Examples are inspection, technical review and walkthrough.
Process area	A cluster of related practices in an area that, when implemented collectively, satisfy a set of goals considered important for making improvements in that area. [CMMI DEV]
Product risk	A risk directly related to the test object.
Product risk assessment	The process of analyzing the product to be tested with the aim of achieving a joint view, for the test manager and other stakeholders, of the more or less risky characteristics and parts of the product to be tested so that the thoroughness of testing can be related to this view. [TMapNext]
Quality	The degree to which a component, system or process meets specified requirements and/or user/customer needs and expectations. [After IEEE 610]
Quality attribute	A feature or characteristic that affects an item's quality. [IEEE 610]

Quality policy	Overall intensions and direction of an organization related to quality as formally expressed by top management. [ISO 9000]
Requirement	A condition or capability needed by a user to solve a problem or achieve an objective that must be met or possessed by a system or system component to satisfy a contract, standard, specification, or other formally imposed document. [After IEEE 610]
Requirements development	The process for eliciting and analyzing the needs of stakeholders and translating those needs into specified product requirements.
Requirements management	The process for managing the requirements of the project's products and to identify inconsistencies between those requirements and the project's plans and work products.
Resumption criteria	The testing activities that must be repeated when testing is re-started after a suspension. [After IEEE 829]
Review	An evaluation of a product or project status to ascertain discrepancies from planned results and to recommend improvements. Examples include management review, informal review, technical review, inspection, and walkthrough. [After IEEE 1028]
Specific goal	A required model component that describes the unique characteristics that must be present to satisfy the process area. [CMMI DEV]
Specific practice	An expected model component that is considered important in achieving the associated specific goal. The specific practices describe the activities expected to result in achievement of the specific goals of a process area. [CMMI DEV]
Staged representation	A model structure wherein attaining the goals of a set of process areas establishes a maturity level; each level builds a foundation for subsequent levels. [CMMI DEV]
Static testing	Testing of a component or system at specification or implementation level without execution of that software, e.g., reviews or static code analysis.
Sub-practice	An informative model component that provides guidance for interpreting and implementing a specific or generic practice. Sub-practices may be worded

as if prescriptive, but are actually meant only to provide ideas that may be useful for process improvement. [CMMI DEV]

Suspension criteria   The criteria used to (temporarily) stop all or a portion of the testing activities on the test items. [After IEEE 829]

Test approach   The implementation of the test strategy for a specific project. It typically includes the decisions made that consider the (test) project's goal and the risk assessment carried out, starting points regarding the test process, the test design techniques to be applied, exit criteria and test types to be performed.

Test automation   The use of software to perform or support test activities, e.g., test management, test design, test execution and results checking.

Test case   A set of input values, execution preconditions, expected results and execution post conditions, developed for a particular objective or test condition, such as to exercise a particular program path or to verify compliance with a specific requirement. [After IEEE 610]

Test condition   An item or event of a component or system that could be verified by one or more test cases, e.g., a function, transaction, feature, quality attribute, or structural element.

Test data   Data that exists (for example, in a database) before a test is executed, and that affects or is affected by the component or system under test.

Test design specification   A document specifying the test conditions (coverage items) for a test item, the detailed test approach and identifying the associated high level test cases. [After IEEE 829]

Test design technique   Procedure used to derive and/or select test cases.

Test environment   An environment containing hardware, instrumentation, simulators, software tools, and other support elements needed to conduct a test. [After IEEE 610]

Test estimation   The calculated approximation of a result (e.g., effort spent, completion date, costs involved, number of test cases, etc.) which is usable even if input data may be incomplete, uncertain, or noisy.

Test execution	The process of running a test on the component or system under test, producing actual result(s).
Test execution schedule	A scheme for the execution of test procedures. The test procedures are included in the test execution schedule in their context and in the order in which they are to be executed.
Test implementation	The process of developing and prioritizing test procedures, creating test data and, optionally, preparing test harnesses and writing automated test scripts.
Test incident	Any event occurring that requires investigation. [After IEEE 1008]
Test level	A group of test activities that are organized and managed together. A test level is linked to the responsibilities in a project. Examples of test levels are component test, integration test, system test and acceptance test. [After TMap]
Test log	A chronological record of relevant details about the execution of tests. [IEEE 829]
Test objective	A reason or purpose for designing and executing a test.
Test plan	A document describing the scope, approach, resources and schedule of intended test activities. It identifies amongst others test items, the features to be tested, the testing tasks, who will do each task, degree of tester independence, the test environment, the test design techniques and entry and exit criteria to be used, and the rationale for their choice, and any risks requiring contingency planning. It is a record of the test planning process. [After IEEE 829]
Test planning	The activity of establishing or updating a test plan.
Test policy	A high level document describing the principles, approach and major objectives of the organization regarding testing.
Test Process Improvement (TPI)	A continuous framework for test process improvement that describes the key elements of an effective test process, especially targeted at system testing and acceptance testing.
Test procedure specification	A document specifying a sequence of actions for the execution of a test. Also known as test script or manual test script. [After IEEE 829]

Test process assets	Artifacts that relate to describing, implementing and improving test processes. Anything that an organization considers to be usefull in attaining the goals of the process area (e.g., policies, process descriptions, supporting templates and tools)
Test project risk	A risk related to management and control of the (test) project, e.g., lack of staffing, strict deadlines, changing requirements, etc.
Test script	Commonly used to refer to a test procedure specification, especially an automated one.
Test strategy	A high-level description of the test levels to be performed and the testing within those levels for an organization or program (one or more projects).
Test tool	A software product that supports one or more test activities, such as planning and control, specification, building initial files and data, test execution and test analysis. [TMap]
Testing	The process consisting of all lifecycle activities, both static and dynamic, concerned with planning, preparation and evaluation of software products and related work products to determine that they satisfy specified requirements, to demonstrate that they are fit for purpose and to detect defects.
TMMi Assessment Method Application Requirements (TAMAR)	A set of requirements to which TMMi assessment processes need to comply. Only formal assessments that have conducted by an assessment method can result in a formal determination of a TMMi level. Note that assessment methods are accredited by the TMMi Foundation based on TAMAR.
Validation	Confirmation by examination and through provision of objective evidence that the requirements for a specific intended use or application have been fulfilled. [ISO 9000]
Verification	Confirmation by examination and through provision of objective evidence that specified requirements have been fulfilled. [ISO 9000]
White-box testing	Testing based on an analysis of the internal structure of the component or system.

About the Authors

Erik van Veenendaal

Drs. Erik van Veenendaal, CISA, has been working as a practitioner and manager in the IT-industry since 1987. After a career in software development, he transferred to the area of software quality. As a test analyst, test manager and test consultant, Erik has over 20 years of practical testing experience. He has implemented structured testing, formal reviews and requirements processes, and has carried out test process improvement activities based on TMMi in a large number of organizations in different industries. Erik has also been a senior lecturer at the Eindhoven University of Technology, Faculty of Technology Management for almost ten years.

Erik founded Improve Quality Services BV (www.improveqs.nl) back in 1998 as an independent organization that focuses on advanced high quality services. He has been the company director for over 12 years. Under his direction Improve Quality Services (www.improveqs.nl) became a leading testing comp any in The Netherlands. Customers are especially to be found in the areas of embedded software (e.g. Philips, Océ en Assembléon) and in the finance domain (e.g. Rabobank, ING and Triodos Bank). Improve Quality Services offers international consultancy and training services with respect to testing (e.g., test process improvement using the TMMi framework), quality management and requirements engineering. Improve Quality Services BV was the second world-wide company to become accredited to perform TMMi assessments. They are a market leader for ISTQB Foundation and ISTQB Advanced training courses and a member of the International Requirements Engineering Board (IREB).

Erik is the (co-)author of numerous papers and a number of books on software quality and testing, including the best-sellers *The Testing Practitioner*, *Foundations of Software Testing* and *Testing according to TMap*. Erik was the first person to receive the ISEB Practitioner certificate with distinction and is also a Certified Information Systems Auditor (CISA). He is a regular speaker both at national and international testing conferences and a leading international trainer (ISTQB accredited) in the field of software testing. At EuroStar'99 (Usability testing), EuroStar'02 (Test Strategies and Planning) and EuroStar'05 (Inspection Leader), he received the best tutorial award.

He is a former vice president of the International Software Testing Qualification Board (ISTQB) (from 2005 – 2009). He is the editor of the ISTQB "Standard Glossary of Terms Used in Software Testing" and vice-chair/

chair of the ISTQB expert level working party since its inception in 2002. Erik is one of the founders of the TMMi Foundation and is currently the vice chair of the TMMi Foundation. He is the lead author of the TMMi model. Erik is actively involved in various working parties of the International Requirements Engineering Board (IREB). For his outstanding contribution to the field of testing Erik received the *"European Testing Excellence Award"* in December, 2007.

After having provided leadership to Improve Quality Services BV for over 12 years,Erik stepped down from that role in July 2010. Since that time he is living in Bonaire where Erik is involved in international test consultancy, training and international organizations (e.g., ISTQB, TMMi and IREB), publications and presentations. As a major shareholder, Erik will remain involved in Improve Quality Services. Erik can be contacted via eve@improveqs.nl or through his website www.erikvanveenendaal.nl.

Jan Jaap Cannegieter

Drs. H.J.J. (Jan Jaap) Cannegieter graduated in 1993 as a Business Economist from the University of Amsterdam. He started his career implementing various automated systems. When he discovered that the quality of the delivered systems was often poor, he turned his interest to testing and quality assurance. Jan Jaap has held various positions involving:

- Structured testing, including test coordination, test management and test consultancy
- Auditing and quick scans
- Reviews and inspections
- Quality assurance in projects
- Implementing CMM(I)
- Process improvement
- Change management
- Requirements development, requirements validation and requirements management.

Examples of organizations in which Jan Jaap has been active include local government agencies, Dutch Tax Administration, various ministries, the Netherlands Chamber of Commerce, Postbank / ING, Rabobank, ABN AMRO, Corus, Central Book house, Swiss Life, Cordares, Achmea Mortgage, Dutch National Railway, KPN, Tele2 and Ziggo.

In addition to his consulting positions, Jan Jaap delivers courses and workshops in Quality Assurance in ICT and requirements. He regularly publishes articles in journals such as *AutomatiseringGids* and *Informatie*, lectures at various universities and colleges and speaks at (international) conferences such as *Testnet, ESEPG, SPIder, PROFES, Dutch Testing Day, LaQuSo* and *Prince 2 User Group*. Jan Jaap is also author of the Dutch books *Kwaliteitszorg in ICT-projecten, Software Process Improvement, De kleine CMMI voor ontwikkeling, De kleine CMMI voor acquisitie, De kleine CMMI voor diensten, Succes met de requirements!, Reviews in de praktijk* and *De kleine TMMi.* Jan Jaap is also co-author of the SEI Technical Note *'CMMI Roadmaps'.* As a member of the development group for TMMi Level 4 and 5, Jan Jaap worked on the process areas Software Quality Evaluation, Advanced Peer Reviews and Defect Prevention.

At the time of publication of this book Jan Jaap is member of the executive board of SYSQA B.V., an independent organization specializing in requirements, testing, quality assurance and process improvement. Within SYSQA he is responsible for knowledge management, product management and quality management. Jan Jaap can be reached via jcannegieter@sysqa.nl or janjaap@vathorstnet.nl.

About the TMMi Foundation

A number of leading practitioners within the testing industry recognized there was a growing need to define an independent global model to be used to evaluate and measure test processes. Only limited attention is given to testing in the various software process improvement models such as the CMMI and the various "test process capability models" that were available did not seem to satisfy the global requirement sufficiently. Out of these discussions, the TMMi Foundation was inaugurated in 2007 to support the development of TMMi. It was agreed that the model should be in the public domain and have no purely academic or commercial "ownership". The founding directors were Andrew Goslin, Fran O'Hara, Mac Miller, Klaus Olsen, Geoff Thompson, Erik van Veenendaal and Brian Wells. The TMMi Foundation is a "not for profit" organization registered in Dublin, Ireland.

Since its inception, the Foundation has attracted interest from around the world and membership is growing all the time. In parallel, an increasing number of organizations are providing financial and other support to the work of the Foundation. These include organizations in Europe, India and South America.

In 2009, the Foundation expanded its organizational capability by creating a Management Executive committee. Membership of the Management Executive committee is open to all registered members of the Foundation and is determined by membership ballot at the Annual General Meeting. The Management Executive has responsibility for implementing the strategic objectives of the Foundation for the next 12-18 months as set by the Board of Directors.

The stated objectives of the Foundation are the following:
- Identifying and securing the ownership of the TMMi Model standard and the ongoing intellectual property rights
- Defining an international core TMMi Model standard and placing it in the public domain
- Creating and managing an independent, unbiased central test maturity data repository
- Provisioning an independent accreditation process for TMMi Assessment Methods based on the standard Model
- Provisioning an independent mechanism to facilitate verification and formal ratification of TMMi Assessment Ratings
- Defining and maintaining independent assessor training, accreditation, guidelines and examinations

- Provisioning a public forum for interested parties to facilitate free interchange of information, education, ideas and usage of the public standard.

To satisfy these objectives, the TMMi Foundation aims to provide the following:
- A standard TMMi Model that can be used in isolation or in support of other process improvement models
- An independently managed data repository to support TMMi assessment method accreditation, assessor and assessment certification/validation and validated assessment data and certificates
- Assessment Method Accreditation/Audit Framework for TMMi in accordance with ISO15504 and the process to certify commercial assessment methods against the standard model.
- Certification and training/examination process, procedures and standards for formal, public accreditation of Assessors and Lead Assessors and the on-going management of these.

Through the Foundation, the testing community (via the technical drafting work groups and the extensive Review Panel membership) is assisting in creating and maintaining its improvement model: the Test Maturity Model Integration (TMMi). The TMMi model is a detailed model for test process capability measurement and the identification of improvements. It is complementary to CMMI but equally supports other software engineering models such as ITIL, ISO 9000 etc.

In 2008, the Foundation also published its TMMi Assessment Method Accreditation Requirements (TAMAR). These are based on ISO15504 and define the requirements of an assessment method package that, if satisfied, will allow the supplier to have the method certified (accredited) by the Foundation. Going forward, the Foundation is looking to provide its own assessment method package for use by organizations as well as providing training.

In parallel with the publication of TAMAR, the Foundation also published criteria and procedures for Assessors and Lead Assessors to be accredited with the Foundation as having the necessary knowledge, training and skills to undertake assessments.

The TMMI Foundation provides published requirements based on a common, global framework which comprises a standard to be used to evaluate and compare test processes.. In addition to this standard reference model, the TMMi Foundation also provides services to publicly accredit methods and assessor resources, This makes it is easier for organizations to assess, measure and compare their processes against a public domain standard that is robust,and widely-accepted.

Full information on the activities, work, accredited TMMi assessment services providers, and publications of the Foundation can be found on our website www.tmmifoundation.org.

Index

Printed in Great Britain
by Amazon